PLANGONOLOGIST LOG BOOK

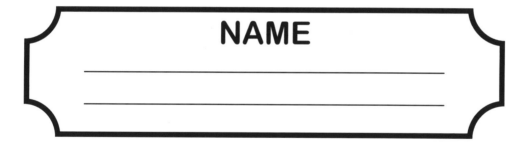

NAME

_____

_____

ADD A PHOTO

BASIC INFORMATIONS

DOLL NAME	COUNTRY OF ORIGIN
MANUFACTURER	YEAR OF PRODUCTION
PURCHASE ☐	GIFT ☐
PURCHASE FROM	GIFT FROM
PURCHASE DATE	GIFT DATE

MARKINGS AND LABELS

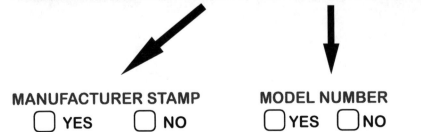

MANUFACTURER STAMP
☐ YES ☐ NO

MODEL NUMBER
☐ YES ☐ NO

SYMBOL
☐ YES  ☐ NO

CONDITION

IT HAS BEEN RESTORED OR REPAIR
YES ☐ NO ☐

CHIPPED
YES ☐ NO ☐

DULL
YES ☐ NO ☐

OTHER SIGNS OF WEAR
YES ☐ NO ☐

COST_____ CURRENT VALUE _____ RARENESS ☆☆☆☆☆

CERTIFICATE OF AUTHENTICITY
YES ☐ NO ☐

CHARACTERISTICS

HEAD_____ HEIGHT_____ ARMS_____

EYE STYLE_____ WEIGHT_____ BODY/SKIN_____

EYE COLOR_____ MOTION_____ HAIR COLOR_____

HAIR TYPE

CARACUL (WOOL) ☐

HUMAN HAIR ☐

MOHAIR ☐

SYNTHETIC HAIR ☐

YARN HAIR ☐

CLOTHES

CLOTHING STYLE_____ FABRIC_____

ACCESSORIES_____

DESCRIPTION OF CLOTHING_____

_____

DOLL CATEGORY

BY TYPE

ADVERTISING DOLLS ⬜	BOUDOIR DOLLS ⬜	MAMA DOLLS ⬜
ANTIQUE LADY DOLLS ⬜	CARNIVAL DOLLS ⬜	MASK FACE DOLLS ⬜
AUTOMATA DOLLS ⬜	DRESS ME DOLLS ⬜	ORIENTAL DOLLS ⬜
BARBIE DOLLS ⬜	GOOGLY EYE DOLLS ⬜	PATSY TYPE DOLLS ⬜
BLACK DOLLS ⬜	KEWPIE DOLLS ⬜	PORCELAIN COLLECTOR ⬜

BY MATERIAL

BISQUE ⬜	COMPOSITION ⬜	RUBBER ⬜
CELLULOID ⬜	HARD PLASTIC ⬜	WAX ⬜
CHINA ⬜	METAL ⬜	WOOD ⬜
CLOTH ⬜	PAPIER MACHE ⬜	

BY COUNTRY

AMERICAN ⬜	FRENCH ⬜	REST OF WORLD ⬜
ENGLISH ⬜	GERMAN ⬜	

ADDITIONAL NOTES

_____

_____

_____

_____

ADD A PHOTO

BASIC INFORMATIONS

DOLL NAME	COUNTRY OF ORIGIN
MANUFACTURER	YEAR OF PRODUCTION
PURCHASE ☐	GIFT ☐
PURCHASE FROM	GIFT FROM
PURCHASE DATE	GIFT DATE

MARKINGS AND LABELS

MANUFACTURER STAMP
☐ YES   ☐ NO

MODEL NUMBER
☐ YES ☐ NO

SYMBOL
☐ YES ☐ NO

CONDITION

IT HAS BEEN RESTORED OR REPAIR YES ☐ NO ☐

CHIPPED YES ☐ NO ☐   DULL YES ☐ NO ☐   OTHER SIGNS OF WEAR YES ☐ NO ☐

COST_____   CURRENT VALUE _____   RARENESS ☆☆☆☆☆

CERTIFICATE OF AUTHENTICITY YES ☐ NO ☐

CHARACTERISTICS

HEAD_____   HEIGHT_____   ARMS_____

EYE STYLE_____   WEIGHT_____   BODY/SKIN_____

EYE COLOR_____   MOTION_____   HAIR COLOR_____

HAIR TYPE

CARACUL (WOOL) ☐

HUMAN HAIR ☐

MOHAIR ☐

SYNTHETIC HAIR ☐

YARN HAIR ☐

CLOTHES

CLOTHING STYLE_____   FABRIC_____

ACCESSORIES_____

DESCRIPTION OF CLOTHING_____

_____

DOLL CATEGORY

BY TYPE

ADVERTISING DOLLS	☐	BOUDOIR DOLLS	☐	MAMA DOLLS	☐
ANTIQUE LADY DOLLS	☐	CARNIVAL DOLLS	☐	MASK FACE DOLLS	☐
AUTOMATA DOLLS	☐	DRESS ME DOLLS	☐	ORIENTAL DOLLS	☐
BARBIE DOLLS	☐	GOOGLY EYE DOLLS	☐	PATSY TYPE DOLLS	☐
BLACK DOLLS	☐	KEWPIE DOLLS	☐	PORCELAIN COLLECTOR	☐

BY MATERIAL

BISQUE	☐	COMPOSITION	☐	RUBBER	☐
CELLULOID	☐	HARD PLASTIC	☐	WAX	☐
CHINA	☐	METAL	☐	WOOD	☐
CLOTH	☐	PAPIER MACHE	☐		

BY COUNTRY

AMERICAN	☐	FRENCH	☐	REST OF WORLD	☐
ENGLISH	☐	GERMAN	☐		

ADDITIONAL NOTES

_____

_____

_____

_____

ADD A PHOTO

BASIC INFORMATIONS

DOLL NAME	COUNTRY OF ORIGIN
MANUFACTURER	YEAR OF PRODUCTION
PURCHASE ☐	GIFT ☐
PURCHASE FROM	GIFT FROM
PURCHASE DATE	GIFT DATE

MARKINGS AND LABELS

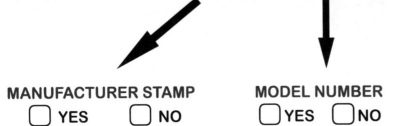

MANUFACTURER STAMP
☐ YES ☐ NO

MODEL NUMBER
☐ YES ☐ NO

SYMBOL
☐ YES ☐ NO

CONDITION

IT HAS BEEN RESTORED OR REPAIR   YES ☐   NO ☐

CHIPPED   YES ☐   NO ☐   DULL   YES ☐   NO ☐   OTHER SIGNS OF WEAR   YES ☐   NO ☐

COST_____   CURRENT VALUE _____   RARENESS ☆☆☆☆☆

CERTIFICATE OF AUTHENTICITY   YES ☐   NO ☐

CHARACTERISTICS

HEAD_____   HEIGHT_____   ARMS_____

EYE STYLE_____   WEIGHT_____   BODY/SKIN_____

EYE COLOR_____   MOTION_____   HAIR COLOR_____

HAIR TYPE

CARACUL (WOOL) ☐

HUMAN HAIR ☐

MOHAIR ☐

SYNTHETIC HAIR ☐

YARN HAIR ☐

CLOTHES

CLOTHING STYLE_____   FABRIC_____

ACCESSORIES_____

DESCRIPTION OF CLOTHING_____

_____

DOLL CATEGORY

BY TYPE

ADVERTISING DOLLS ☐	BOUDOIR DOLLS ☐	MAMA DOLLS ☐
ANTIQUE LADY DOLLS ☐	CARNIVAL DOLLS ☐	MASK FACE DOLLS ☐
AUTOMATA DOLLS ☐	DRESS ME DOLLS ☐	ORIENTAL DOLLS ☐
BARBIE DOLLS ☐	GOOGLY EYE DOLLS ☐	PATSY TYPE DOLLS ☐
BLACK DOLLS ☐	KEWPIE DOLLS ☐	PORCELAIN COLLECTOR ☐

BY MATERIAL

BISQUE ☐	COMPOSITION ☐	RUBBER ☐
CELLULOID ☐	HARD PLASTIC ☐	WAX ☐
CHINA ☐	METAL ☐	WOOD ☐
CLOTH ☐	PAPIER MACHE ☐	

BY COUNTRY

AMERICAN ☐	FRENCH ☐	REST OF WORLD ☐
ENGLISH ☐	GERMAN ☐	

ADDITIONAL NOTES

_____

_____

_____

_____

ADD A PHOTO

BASIC INFORMATIONS

DOLL NAME	COUNTRY OF ORIGIN
MANUFACTURER	YEAR OF PRODUCTION
PURCHASE ☐	GIFT ☐
PURCHASE FROM	GIFT FROM
PURCHASE DATE	GIFT DATE

MARKINGS AND LABELS

MANUFACTURER STAMP
☐ YES ☐ NO

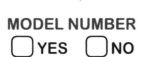

MODEL NUMBER
☐ YES ☐ NO

SYMBOL
☐ YES ☐ NO

CONDITION

IT HAS BEEN RESTORED OR REPAIR YES ☐ NO ☐

CHIPPED YES ☐ NO ☐   DULL YES ☐ NO ☐   OTHER SIGNS OF WEAR YES ☐ NO ☐

COST_____   CURRENT VALUE _____   RARENESS ☆☆☆☆☆

CERTIFICATE OF AUTHENTICITY YES ☐ NO ☐

CHARACTERISTICS

HEAD_____   HEIGHT_____   ARMS_____

EYE STYLE_____   WEIGHT_____   BODY/SKIN_____

EYE COLOR_____   MOTION_____   HAIR COLOR_____

HAIR TYPE

CARACUL (WOOL) ☐

HUMAN HAIR ☐

MOHAIR ☐

SYNTHETIC HAIR ☐

YARN HAIR ☐

CLOTHES

CLOTHING STYLE_____   FABRIC_____

ACCESSORIES_____

DESCRIPTION OF CLOTHING_____

_____

DOLL CATEGORY

BY TYPE

ADVERTISING DOLLS	☐	BOUDOIR DOLLS	☐	MAMA DOLLS	☐
ANTIQUE LADY DOLLS	☐	CARNIVAL DOLLS	☐	MASK FACE DOLLS	☐
AUTOMATA DOLLS	☐	DRESS ME DOLLS	☐	ORIENTAL DOLLS	☐
BARBIE DOLLS	☐	GOOGLY EYE DOLLS	☐	PATSY TYPE DOLLS	☐
BLACK DOLLS	☐	KEWPIE DOLLS	☐	PORCELAIN COLLECTOR	☐

BY MATERIAL

BISQUE	☐	COMPOSITION	☐	RUBBER	☐
CELLULOID	☐	HARD PLASTIC	☐	WAX	☐
CHINA	☐	METAL	☐	WOOD	☐
CLOTH	☐	PAPIER MACHE	☐		

BY COUNTRY

AMERICAN	☐	FRENCH	☐	REST OF WORLD	☐
ENGLISH	☐	GERMAN	☐		

ADDITIONAL NOTES

_____

_____

_____

_____

ADD A PHOTO

BASIC INFORMATIONS

DOLL NAME	COUNTRY OF ORIGIN
MANUFACTURER	YEAR OF PRODUCTION
PURCHASE ☐	GIFT ☐
PURCHASE FROM	GIFT FROM
PURCHASE DATE	GIFT DATE

MARKINGS AND LABELS

MANUFACTURER STAMP	MODEL NUMBER	SYMBOL
☐ YES ☐ NO	☐ YES ☐ NO	☐ YES ☐ NO

CONDITION

IT HAS BEEN RESTORED OR REPAIR YES ☐ NO ☐

CHIPPED YES ☐ NO ☐   DULL YES ☐ NO ☐   OTHER SIGNS OF WEAR YES ☐ NO ☐

COST_____   CURRENT VALUE _____   RARENESS ☆☆☆☆☆

CERTIFICATE OF AUTHENTICITY YES ☐ NO ☐

CHARACTERISTICS

HEAD_____   HEIGHT_____   ARMS_____

EYE STYLE_____   WEIGHT_____   BODY/SKIN_____

EYE COLOR_____   MOTION_____   HAIR COLOR_____

HAIR TYPE

CARACUL (WOOL) ☐

HUMAN HAIR ☐

MOHAIR ☐

SYNTHETIC HAIR ☐

YARN HAIR ☐

CLOTHES

CLOTHING STYLE_____   FABRIC_____

ACCESSORIES_____

DESCRIPTION OF CLOTHING_____

_____

DOLL CATEGORY

BY TYPE

ADVERTISING DOLLS ☐	BOUDOIR DOLLS ☐	MAMA DOLLS ☐
ANTIQUE LADY DOLLS ☐	CARNIVAL DOLLS ☐	MASK FACE DOLLS ☐
AUTOMATA DOLLS ☐	DRESS ME DOLLS ☐	ORIENTAL DOLLS ☐
BARBIE DOLLS ☐	GOOGLY EYE DOLLS ☐	PATSY TYPE DOLLS ☐
BLACK DOLLS ☐	KEWPIE DOLLS ☐	PORCELAIN COLLECTOR ☐

BY MATERIAL

BISQUE ☐	COMPOSITION ☐	RUBBER ☐
CELLULOID ☐	HARD PLASTIC ☐	WAX ☐
CHINA ☐	METAL ☐	WOOD ☐
CLOTH ☐	PAPIER MACHE ☐	

BY COUNTRY

AMERICAN ☐	FRENCH ☐	REST OF WORLD ☐
ENGLISH ☐	GERMAN ☐	

ADDITIONAL NOTES

_____

_____

_____

_____

ADD A PHOTO

BASIC INFORMATIONS

DOLL NAME	COUNTRY OF ORIGIN
MANUFACTURER	YEAR OF PRODUCTION
PURCHASE ☐	GIFT ☐
PURCHASE FROM	GIFT FROM
PURCHASE DATE	GIFT DATE

MARKINGS AND LABELS

MANUFACTURER STAMP
☐ YES   ☐ NO

MODEL NUMBER
☐ YES ☐ NO

SYMBOL
☐ YES   ☐ NO

CONDITION

IT HAS BEEN RESTORED OR REPAIR   YES ☐ NO ☐

CHIPPED   YES ☐ NO ☐   DULL   YES ☐ NO ☐   OTHER SIGNS OF WEAR   YES ☐ NO ☐

COST_____   CURRENT VALUE _____   RARENESS ☆☆☆☆☆

CERTIFICATE OF AUTHENTICITY   YES ☐ NO ☐

CHARACTERISTICS

HEAD_____   HEIGHT_____   ARMS_____

EYE STYLE_____   WEIGHT_____   BODY/SKIN_____

EYE COLOR_____   MOTION_____   HAIR COLOR_____

HAIR TYPE

CARACUL (WOOL) ☐

HUMAN HAIR ☐

MOHAIR ☐

SYNTHETIC HAIR ☐

YARN HAIR ☐

CLOTHES

CLOTHING STYLE_____   FABRIC_____

ACCESSORIES_____

DESCRIPTION OF CLOTHING_____

_____

DOLL CATEGORY

BY TYPE

ADVERTISING DOLLS	☐	BOUDOIR DOLLS	☐	MAMA DOLLS	☐
ANTIQUE LADY DOLLS	☐	CARNIVAL DOLLS	☐	MASK FACE DOLLS	☐
AUTOMATA DOLLS	☐	DRESS ME DOLLS	☐	ORIENTAL DOLLS	☐
BARBIE DOLLS	☐	GOOGLY EYE DOLLS	☐	PATSY TYPE DOLLS	☐
BLACK DOLLS	☐	KEWPIE DOLLS	☐	PORCELAIN COLLECTOR	☐

BY MATERIAL

BISQUE	☐	COMPOSITION	☐	RUBBER	☐
CELLULOID	☐	HARD PLASTIC	☐	WAX	☐
CHINA	☐	METAL	☐	WOOD	☐
CLOTH	☐	PAPIER MACHE	☐		

BY COUNTRY

AMERICAN	☐	FRENCH	☐	REST OF WORLD	☐
ENGLISH	☐	GERMAN	☐		

ADDITIONAL NOTES

_____

_____

_____

_____

ADD A PHOTO

BASIC INFORMATIONS

DOLL NAME	COUNTRY OF ORIGIN
MANUFACTURER	YEAR OF PRODUCTION
PURCHASE ☐	GIFT ☐
PURCHASE FROM	GIFT FROM
PURCHASE DATE	GIFT DATE

MARKINGS AND LABELS

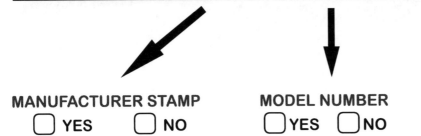

MANUFACTURER STAMP
☐ YES ☐ NO

MODEL NUMBER
☐ YES ☐ NO

SYMBOL
☐ YES ☐ NO

CONDITION

IT HAS BEEN RESTORED OR REPAIR   YES ☐   NO ☐

CHIPPED   YES ☐   NO ☐   DULL   YES ☐   NO ☐   OTHER SIGNS OF WEAR   YES ☐   NO ☐

COST_____   CURRENT VALUE _____   RARENESS ☆☆☆☆☆

CERTIFICATE OF AUTHENTICITY   YES ☐   NO ☐

CHARACTERISTICS

HEAD_____   HEIGHT_____   ARMS_____

EYE STYLE_____   WEIGHT_____   BODY/SKIN_____

EYE COLOR_____   MOTION_____   HAIR COLOR_____

HAIR TYPE

CARACUL (WOOL) ☐

HUMAN HAIR ☐

MOHAIR ☐

SYNTHETIC HAIR ☐

YARN HAIR ☐

CLOTHES

CLOTHING STYLE_____   FABRIC_____

ACCESSORIES_____

DESCRIPTION OF CLOTHING_____

_____

DOLL CATEGORY

BY TYPE

ADVERTISING DOLLS ☐	BOUDOIR DOLLS ☐	MAMA DOLLS ☐
ANTIQUE LADY DOLLS ☐	CARNIVAL DOLLS ☐	MASK FACE DOLLS ☐
AUTOMATA DOLLS ☐	DRESS ME DOLLS ☐	ORIENTAL DOLLS ☐
BARBIE DOLLS ☐	GOOGLY EYE DOLLS ☐	PATSY TYPE DOLLS ☐
BLACK DOLLS ☐	KEWPIE DOLLS ☐	PORCELAIN COLLECTOR ☐

BY MATERIAL

BISQUE ☐	COMPOSITION ☐	RUBBER ☐
CELLULOID ☐	HARD PLASTIC ☐	WAX ☐
CHINA ☐	METAL ☐	WOOD ☐
CLOTH ☐	PAPIER MACHE ☐	

BY COUNTRY

AMERICAN ☐	FRENCH ☐	REST OF WORLD ☐
ENGLISH ☐	GERMAN ☐	

ADDITIONAL NOTES

_____

_____

_____

_____

ADD A PHOTO

BASIC INFORMATIONS

DOLL NAME	COUNTRY OF ORIGIN
MANUFACTURER	YEAR OF PRODUCTION
PURCHASE ☐	GIFT ☐
PURCHASE FROM	GIFT FROM
PURCHASE DATE	GIFT DATE

MARKINGS AND LABELS

MANUFACTURER STAMP
☐ YES ☐ NO

MODEL NUMBER
☐ YES ☐ NO

SYMBOL
☐ YES ☐ NO

CONDITION

IT HAS BEEN RESTORED OR REPAIR YES ☐ NO ☐

CHIPPED YES ☐ NO ☐   DULL YES ☐ NO ☐   OTHER SIGNS OF WEAR YES ☐ NO ☐

COST_____   CURRENT VALUE _____   RARENESS ☆☆☆☆☆

CERTIFICATE OF AUTHENTICITY YES ☐ NO ☐

CHARACTERISTICS

HEAD_____   HEIGHT_____   ARMS_____

EYE STYLE_____   WEIGHT_____   BODY/SKIN_____

EYE COLOR_____   MOTION_____   HAIR COLOR_____

HAIR TYPE

CARACUL (WOOL) ☐

HUMAN HAIR ☐

MOHAIR ☐

SYNTHETIC HAIR ☐

YARN HAIR ☐

CLOTHES

CLOTHING STYLE_____   FABRIC_____

ACCESSORIES_____

DESCRIPTION OF CLOTHING_____

_____

DOLL CATEGORY

BY TYPE

ADVERTISING DOLLS ☐	BOUDOIR DOLLS ☐	MAMA DOLLS ☐
ANTIQUE LADY DOLLS ☐	CARNIVAL DOLLS ☐	MASK FACE DOLLS ☐
AUTOMATA DOLLS ☐	DRESS ME DOLLS ☐	ORIENTAL DOLLS ☐
BARBIE DOLLS ☐	GOOGLY EYE DOLLS ☐	PATSY TYPE DOLLS ☐
BLACK DOLLS ☐	KEWPIE DOLLS ☐	PORCELAIN COLLECTOR ☐

BY MATERIAL

BISQUE ☐	COMPOSITION ☐	RUBBER ☐
CELLULOID ☐	HARD PLASTIC ☐	WAX ☐
CHINA ☐	METAL ☐	WOOD ☐
CLOTH ☐	PAPIER MACHE ☐	

BY COUNTRY

AMERICAN ☐	FRENCH ☐	REST OF WORLD ☐
ENGLISH ☐	GERMAN ☐	

ADDITIONAL NOTES

_____

_____

_____

_____

ADD A PHOTO

BASIC INFORMATIONS

DOLL NAME	COUNTRY OF ORIGIN
MANUFACTURER	YEAR OF PRODUCTION
PURCHASE ☐	GIFT ☐
PURCHASE FROM	GIFT FROM
PURCHASE DATE	GIFT DATE

MARKINGS AND LABELS

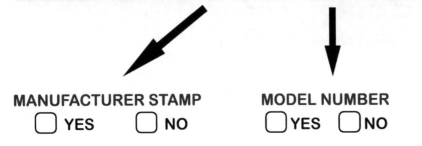

MANUFACTURER STAMP
☐ YES   ☐ NO

MODEL NUMBER
☐ YES ☐ NO

SYMBOL
☐ YES ☐ NO

CONDITION

IT HAS BEEN RESTORED OR REPAIR   YES ☐   NO ☐

CHIPPED   YES ☐   NO ☐   DULL   YES ☐   NO ☐   OTHER SIGNS OF WEAR   YES ☐   NO ☐

COST_____   CURRENT VALUE _____   RARENESS ☆☆☆☆☆

CERTIFICATE OF AUTHENTICITY   YES ☐   NO ☐

CHARACTERISTICS

HEAD_____   HEIGHT_____   ARMS_____

EYE STYLE_____   WEIGHT_____   BODY/SKIN_____

EYE COLOR_____   MOTION_____   HAIR COLOR_____

HAIR TYPE

CARACUL (WOOL) ☐

HUMAN HAIR ☐

MOHAIR ☐

SYNTHETIC HAIR ☐

YARN HAIR ☐

CLOTHES

CLOTHING STYLE_____   FABRIC_____

ACCESSORIES_____

DESCRIPTION OF CLOTHING_____

_____

DOLL CATEGORY

BY TYPE

ADVERTISING DOLLS ☐	BOUDOIR DOLLS ☐	MAMA DOLLS ☐
ANTIQUE LADY DOLLS ☐	CARNIVAL DOLLS ☐	MASK FACE DOLLS ☐
AUTOMATA DOLLS ☐	DRESS ME DOLLS ☐	ORIENTAL DOLLS ☐
BARBIE DOLLS ☐	GOOGLY EYE DOLLS ☐	PATSY TYPE DOLLS ☐
BLACK DOLLS ☐	KEWPIE DOLLS ☐	PORCELAIN COLLECTOR ☐

BY MATERIAL

BISQUE ☐	COMPOSITION ☐	RUBBER ☐
CELLULOID ☐	HARD PLASTIC ☐	WAX ☐
CHINA ☐	METAL ☐	WOOD ☐
CLOTH ☐	PAPIER MACHE ☐	

BY COUNTRY

AMERICAN ☐	FRENCH ☐	REST OF WORLD ☐
ENGLISH ☐	GERMAN ☐	

ADDITIONAL NOTES

_____

_____

_____

_____

ADD A PHOTO

BASIC INFORMATIONS

DOLL NAME	COUNTRY OF ORIGIN
MANUFACTURER	YEAR OF PRODUCTION
PURCHASE ☐	GIFT ☐
PURCHASE FROM	GIFT FROM
PURCHASE DATE	GIFT DATE

MARKINGS AND LABELS

MANUFACTURER STAMP
☐ YES ☐ NO

MODEL NUMBER
☐ YES ☐ NO

SYMBOL
☐ YES ☐ NO

CONDITION

IT HAS BEEN RESTORED OR REPAIR
YES ☐ NO ☐

CHIPPED YES ☐ NO ☐

DULL YES ☐ NO ☐

OTHER SIGNS OF WEAR YES ☐ NO ☐

COST_____   CURRENT VALUE _____   RARENESS ★★★★☆

CERTIFICATE OF AUTHENTICITY YES ☐ NO ☐

CHARACTERISTICS

HEAD_____   HEIGHT_____   ARMS_____

EYE STYLE_____   WEIGHT_____   BODY/SKIN_____

EYE COLOR_____   MOTION_____   HAIR COLOR_____

HAIR TYPE

CARACUL (WOOL) ☐

HUMAN HAIR ☐

MOHAIR ☐

SYNTHETIC HAIR ☐

YARN HAIR ☐

CLOTHES

CLOTHING STYLE_____   FABRIC_____

ACCESSORIES_____

DESCRIPTION OF CLOTHING_____

_____

DOLL CATEGORY

BY TYPE

ADVERTISING DOLLS ☐	BOUDOIR DOLLS ☐	MAMA DOLLS ☐
ANTIQUE LADY DOLLS ☐	CARNIVAL DOLLS ☐	MASK FACE DOLLS ☐
AUTOMATA DOLLS ☐	DRESS ME DOLLS ☐	ORIENTAL DOLLS ☐
BARBIE DOLLS ☐	GOOGLY EYE DOLLS ☐	PATSY TYPE DOLLS ☐
BLACK DOLLS ☐	KEWPIE DOLLS ☐	PORCELAIN COLLECTOR ☐

BY MATERIAL

BISQUE ☐	COMPOSITION ☐	RUBBER ☐
CELLULOID ☐	HARD PLASTIC ☐	WAX ☐
CHINA ☐	METAL ☐	WOOD ☐
CLOTH ☐	PAPIER MACHE ☐	

BY COUNTRY

AMERICAN ☐	FRENCH ☐	REST OF WORLD ☐
ENGLISH ☐	GERMAN ☐	

ADDITIONAL NOTES

_____

_____

_____

_____

ADD A PHOTO

BASIC INFORMATIONS

DOLL NAME	COUNTRY OF ORIGIN
MANUFACTURER	YEAR OF PRODUCTION
PURCHASE ☐	GIFT ☐
PURCHASE FROM	GIFT FROM
PURCHASE DATE	GIFT DATE

MARKINGS AND LABELS

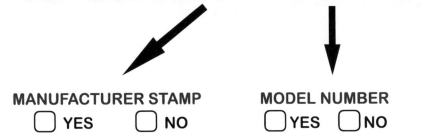

MANUFACTURER STAMP	MODEL NUMBER	SYMBOL
☐ YES ☐ NO	☐ YES ☐ NO	☐ YES ☐ NO

CONDITION

IT HAS BEEN RESTORED OR REPAIR YES ☐ NO ☐

CHIPPED YES ☐ NO ☐   DULL YES ☐ NO ☐   OTHER SIGNS OF WEAR YES ☐ NO ☐

COST_____   CURRENT VALUE _____   RARENESS ☆☆☆☆☆

CERTIFICATE OF AUTHENTICITY YES ☐ NO ☐

CHARACTERISTICS

HEAD_____   HEIGHT_____   ARMS_____

EYE STYLE_____   WEIGHT_____   BODY/SKIN_____

EYE COLOR_____   MOTION_____   HAIR COLOR_____

HAIR TYPE

CARACUL (WOOL) ☐

HUMAN HAIR ☐

MOHAIR ☐

SYNTHETIC HAIR ☐

YARN HAIR ☐

CLOTHES

CLOTHING STYLE_____   FABRIC_____

ACCESSORIES_____

DESCRIPTION OF CLOTHING_____

_____

DOLL CATEGORY

BY TYPE

ADVERTISING DOLLS ☐	BOUDOIR DOLLS ☐	MAMA DOLLS ☐
ANTIQUE LADY DOLLS ☐	CARNIVAL DOLLS ☐	MASK FACE DOLLS ☐
AUTOMATA DOLLS ☐	DRESS ME DOLLS ☐	ORIENTAL DOLLS ☐
BARBIE DOLLS ☐	GOOGLY EYE DOLLS ☐	PATSY TYPE DOLLS ☐
BLACK DOLLS ☐	KEWPIE DOLLS ☐	PORCELAIN COLLECTOR ☐

BY MATERIAL

BISQUE ☐	COMPOSITION ☐	RUBBER ☐
CELLULOID ☐	HARD PLASTIC ☐	WAX ☐
CHINA ☐	METAL ☐	WOOD ☐
CLOTH ☐	PAPIER MACHE ☐	

BY COUNTRY

AMERICAN ☐	FRENCH ☐	REST OF WORLD ☐
ENGLISH ☐	GERMAN ☐	

ADDITIONAL NOTES

_____

_____

_____

_____

ADD A PHOTO

BASIC INFORMATIONS

DOLL NAME		COUNTRY OF ORIGIN
MANUFACTURER		YEAR OF PRODUCTION
PURCHASE ☐		GIFT ☐
PURCHASE FROM		GIFT FROM
PURCHASE DATE		GIFT DATE

MARKINGS AND LABELS

MANUFACTURER STAMP
☐ YES   ☐ NO

MODEL NUMBER
☐ YES   ☐ NO

SYMBOL
☐ YES   ☐ NO

CONDITION

IT HAS BEEN RESTORED OR REPAIR YES ☐ NO ☐

CHIPPED YES ☐ NO ☐   DULL YES ☐ NO ☐   OTHER SIGNS OF WEAR YES ☐ NO ☐

COST _____   CURRENT VALUE _____   RARENESS ☆☆☆☆☆

CERTIFICATE OF AUTHENTICITY YES ☐ NO ☐

CHARACTERISTICS

HEAD _____   HEIGHT _____   ARMS _____

EYE STYLE _____   WEIGHT _____   BODY/SKIN _____

EYE COLOR _____   MOTION _____   HAIR COLOR _____

HAIR TYPE

CARACUL (WOOL) ☐

HUMAN HAIR ☐

MOHAIR ☐

SYNTHETIC HAIR ☐

YARN HAIR ☐

CLOTHES

CLOTHING STYLE _____   FABRIC _____

ACCESSORIES _____

DESCRIPTION OF CLOTHING _____

_____

DOLL CATEGORY

BY TYPE

ADVERTISING DOLLS	☐	BOUDOIR DOLLS	☐	MAMA DOLLS	☐
ANTIQUE LADY DOLLS	☐	CARNIVAL DOLLS	☐	MASK FACE DOLLS	☐
AUTOMATA DOLLS	☐	DRESS ME DOLLS	☐	ORIENTAL DOLLS	☐
BARBIE DOLLS	☐	GOOGLY EYE DOLLS	☐	PATSY TYPE DOLLS	☐
BLACK DOLLS	☐	KEWPIE DOLLS	☐	PORCELAIN COLLECTOR	☐

BY MATERIAL

BISQUE	☐	COMPOSITION	☐	RUBBER	☐
CELLULOID	☐	HARD PLASTIC	☐	WAX	☐
CHINA	☐	METAL	☐	WOOD	☐
CLOTH	☐	PAPIER MACHE	☐		

BY COUNTRY

AMERICAN	☐	FRENCH	☐	REST OF WORLD	☐
ENGLISH	☐	GERMAN	☐		

ADDITIONAL NOTES

_____

_____

_____

_____

ADD A PHOTO

BASIC INFORMATIONS

DOLL NAME	COUNTRY OF ORIGIN
MANUFACTURER	YEAR OF PRODUCTION
PURCHASE ☐	GIFT ☐
PURCHASE FROM	GIFT FROM
PURCHASE DATE	GIFT DATE

MARKINGS AND LABELS

MANUFACTURER STAMP

☐ YES   ☐ NO

MODEL NUMBER

☐ YES ☐ NO

SYMBOL

☐ YES   ☐ NO

CONDITION

IT HAS BEEN RESTORED OR REPAIR   YES ☐   NO ☐

CHIPPED   YES ☐   NO ☐   DULL   YES ☐   NO ☐   OTHER SIGNS OF WEAR   YES ☐   NO ☐

COST_____   CURRENT VALUE _____   RARENESS ☆☆☆☆☆

CERTIFICATE OF AUTHENTICITY   YES ☐   NO ☐

CHARACTERISTICS

HEAD_____   HEIGHT_____   ARMS_____

EYE STYLE_____   WEIGHT_____   BODY/SKIN_____

EYE COLOR_____   MOTION_____   HAIR COLOR_____

HAIR TYPE

CARACUL (WOOL) ☐

HUMAN HAIR ☐

MOHAIR ☐

SYNTHETIC HAIR ☐

YARN HAIR ☐

CLOTHES

CLOTHING STYLE_____   FABRIC_____

ACCESSORIES_____

DESCRIPTION OF CLOTHING_____

_____

DOLL CATEGORY

BY TYPE

ADVERTISING DOLLS ☐	BOUDOIR DOLLS ☐	MAMA DOLLS ☐
ANTIQUE LADY DOLLS ☐	CARNIVAL DOLLS ☐	MASK FACE DOLLS ☐
AUTOMATA DOLLS ☐	DRESS ME DOLLS ☐	ORIENTAL DOLLS ☐
BARBIE DOLLS ☐	GOOGLY EYE DOLLS ☐	PATSY TYPE DOLLS ☐
BLACK DOLLS ☐	KEWPIE DOLLS ☐	PORCELAIN COLLECTOR ☐

BY MATERIAL

BISQUE ☐	COMPOSITION ☐	RUBBER ☐
CELLULOID ☐	HARD PLASTIC ☐	WAX ☐
CHINA ☐	METAL ☐	WOOD ☐
CLOTH ☐	PAPIER MACHE ☐	

BY COUNTRY

AMERICAN ☐	FRENCH ☐	REST OF WORLD ☐
ENGLISH ☐	GERMAN ☐	

ADDITIONAL NOTES

_____

_____

_____

_____

ADD A PHOTO

BASIC INFORMATIONS

DOLL NAME	COUNTRY OF ORIGIN
MANUFACTURER	YEAR OF PRODUCTION
PURCHASE ☐	GIFT ☐
PURCHASE FROM	GIFT FROM
PURCHASE DATE	GIFT DATE

MARKINGS AND LABELS

MANUFACTURER STAMP
☐ YES ☐ NO

MODEL NUMBER
☐ YES ☐ NO

SYMBOL
☐ YES ☐ NO

CONDITION

IT HAS BEEN RESTORED OR REPAIR YES ☐ NO ☐

CHIPPED YES ☐ NO ☐   DULL YES ☐ NO ☐   OTHER SIGNS OF WEAR YES ☐ NO ☐

COST_____   CURRENT VALUE _____   RARENESS ☆☆☆☆☆

CERTIFICATE OF AUTHENTICITY YES ☐ NO ☐

CHARACTERISTICS

HEAD_____   HEIGHT_____   ARMS_____

EYE STYLE_____   WEIGHT_____   BODY/SKIN_____

EYE COLOR_____   MOTION_____   HAIR COLOR_____

HAIR TYPE

CARACUL (WOOL) ☐

HUMAN HAIR ☐

MOHAIR ☐

SYNTHETIC HAIR ☐

YARN HAIR ☐

CLOTHES

CLOTHING STYLE_____   FABRIC_____

ACCESSORIES_____

DESCRIPTION OF CLOTHING_____

_____

DOLL CATEGORY

BY TYPE

ADVERTISING DOLLS ☐	BOUDOIR DOLLS ☐	MAMA DOLLS ☐
ANTIQUE LADY DOLLS ☐	CARNIVAL DOLLS ☐	MASK FACE DOLLS ☐
AUTOMATA DOLLS ☐	DRESS ME DOLLS ☐	ORIENTAL DOLLS ☐
BARBIE DOLLS ☐	GOOGLY EYE DOLLS ☐	PATSY TYPE DOLLS ☐
BLACK DOLLS ☐	KEWPIE DOLLS ☐	PORCELAIN COLLECTOR ☐

BY MATERIAL

BISQUE ☐	COMPOSITION ☐	RUBBER ☐
CELLULOID ☐	HARD PLASTIC ☐	WAX ☐
CHINA ☐	METAL ☐	WOOD ☐
CLOTH ☐	PAPIER MACHE ☐	

BY COUNTRY

AMERICAN ☐	FRENCH ☐	REST OF WORLD ☐
ENGLISH ☐	GERMAN ☐	

ADDITIONAL NOTES

_____

_____

_____

_____

ADD A PHOTO

BASIC INFORMATIONS

DOLL NAME	COUNTRY OF ORIGIN
MANUFACTURER	YEAR OF PRODUCTION
PURCHASE ☐	GIFT ☐
PURCHASE FROM	GIFT FROM
PURCHASE DATE	GIFT DATE

MARKINGS AND LABELS

MANUFACTURER STAMP
☐ YES   ☐ NO

MODEL NUMBER
☐ YES   ☐ NO

SYMBOL
☐ YES   ☐ NO

CONDITION

IT HAS BEEN RESTORED OR REPAIR   YES ☐ NO ☐

CHIPPED YES ☐ NO ☐   DULL YES ☐ NO ☐   OTHER SIGNS OF WEAR YES ☐ NO ☐

COST_____   CURRENT VALUE _____   RARENESS ☆☆☆☆☆

CERTIFICATE OF AUTHENTICITY YES ☐ NO ☐

CHARACTERISTICS

HEAD_____   HEIGHT_____   ARMS_____

EYE STYLE_____   WEIGHT_____   BODY/SKIN_____

EYE COLOR_____   MOTION_____   HAIR COLOR_____

HAIR TYPE

CARACUL (WOOL) ☐

HUMAN HAIR ☐

MOHAIR ☐

SYNTHETIC HAIR ☐

YARN HAIR ☐

CLOTHES

CLOTHING STYLE_____   FABRIC_____

ACCESSORIES_____

DESCRIPTION OF CLOTHING_____

_____

DOLL CATEGORY

BY TYPE

ADVERTISING DOLLS ☐	BOUDOIR DOLLS ☐	MAMA DOLLS ☐
ANTIQUE LADY DOLLS ☐	CARNIVAL DOLLS ☐	MASK FACE DOLLS ☐
AUTOMATA DOLLS ☐	DRESS ME DOLLS ☐	ORIENTAL DOLLS ☐
BARBIE DOLLS ☐	GOOGLY EYE DOLLS ☐	PATSY TYPE DOLLS ☐
BLACK DOLLS ☐	KEWPIE DOLLS ☐	PORCELAIN COLLECTOR ☐

BY MATERIAL

BISQUE ☐	COMPOSITION ☐	RUBBER ☐
CELLULOID ☐	HARD PLASTIC ☐	WAX ☐
CHINA ☐	METAL ☐	WOOD ☐
CLOTH ☐	PAPIER MACHE ☐	

BY COUNTRY

AMERICAN ☐	FRENCH ☐	REST OF WORLD ☐
ENGLISH ☐	GERMAN ☐	

ADDITIONAL NOTES

_____

_____

_____

_____

ADD A PHOTO

BASIC INFORMATIONS

DOLL NAME	COUNTRY OF ORIGIN
MANUFACTURER	YEAR OF PRODUCTION
PURCHASE ☐	GIFT ☐
PURCHASE FROM	GIFT FROM
PURCHASE DATE	GIFT DATE

MARKINGS AND LABELS

MANUFACTURER STAMP
☐ YES ☐ NO

MODEL NUMBER
☐ YES ☐ NO

SYMBOL
☐ YES ☐ NO

CONDITION

IT HAS BEEN RESTORED OR REPAIR   YES ☐ NO ☐

CHIPPED   YES ☐ NO ☐   DULL   YES ☐ NO ☐   OTHER SIGNS OF WEAR   YES ☐ NO ☐

COST_____   CURRENT VALUE _____   RARENESS ☆☆☆☆☆

CERTIFICATE OF AUTHENTICITY   YES ☐ NO ☐

CHARACTERISTICS

HEAD_____   HEIGHT_____   ARMS_____

EYE STYLE_____   WEIGHT_____   BODY/SKIN_____

EYE COLOR_____   MOTION_____   HAIR COLOR_____

HAIR TYPE

CARACUL (WOOL) ☐

HUMAN HAIR ☐

MOHAIR ☐

SYNTHETIC HAIR ☐

YARN HAIR ☐

CLOTHES

CLOTHING STYLE_____   FABRIC_____

ACCESSORIES_____

DESCRIPTION OF CLOTHING_____

_____

DOLL CATEGORY

BY TYPE

ADVERTISING DOLLS ☐	BOUDOIR DOLLS ☐	MAMA DOLLS ☐
ANTIQUE LADY DOLLS ☐	CARNIVAL DOLLS ☐	MASK FACE DOLLS ☐
AUTOMATA DOLLS ☐	DRESS ME DOLLS ☐	ORIENTAL DOLLS ☐
BARBIE DOLLS ☐	GOOGLY EYE DOLLS ☐	PATSY TYPE DOLLS ☐
BLACK DOLLS ☐	KEWPIE DOLLS ☐	PORCELAIN COLLECTOR ☐

BY MATERIAL

BISQUE ☐	COMPOSITION ☐	RUBBER ☐
CELLULOID ☐	HARD PLASTIC ☐	WAX ☐
CHINA ☐	METAL ☐	WOOD ☐
CLOTH ☐	PAPIER MACHE ☐	

BY COUNTRY

AMERICAN ☐	FRENCH ☐	REST OF WORLD ☐
ENGLISH ☐	GERMAN ☐	

ADDITIONAL NOTES

_____

_____

_____

_____

ADD A PHOTO

BASIC INFORMATIONS

DOLL NAME	COUNTRY OF ORIGIN
MANUFACTURER	YEAR OF PRODUCTION
PURCHASE ☐	GIFT ☐
PURCHASE FROM	GIFT FROM
PURCHASE DATE	GIFT DATE

MARKINGS AND LABELS

MANUFACTURER STAMP
☐ YES ☐ NO

MODEL NUMBER
☐ YES ☐ NO

SYMBOL
☐ YES ☐ NO

CONDITION

IT HAS BEEN RESTORED OR REPAIR YES ☐ NO ☐

CHIPPED YES ☐ NO ☐   DULL YES ☐ NO ☐   OTHER SIGNS OF WEAR YES ☐ NO ☐

COST_____   CURRENT VALUE _____   RARENESS ☆☆☆☆☆

CERTIFICATE OF AUTHENTICITY YES ☐ NO ☐

CHARACTERISTICS

HEAD_____   HEIGHT_____   ARMS_____

EYE STYLE_____   WEIGHT_____   BODY/SKIN_____

EYE COLOR_____   MOTION_____   HAIR COLOR_____

HAIR TYPE

CARACUL (WOOL) ☐

HUMAN HAIR ☐

MOHAIR ☐

SYNTHETIC HAIR ☐

YARN HAIR ☐

CLOTHES

CLOTHING STYLE_____   FABRIC_____

ACCESSORIES_____

DESCRIPTION OF CLOTHING_____

_____

DOLL CATEGORY

BY TYPE

ADVERTISING DOLLS ☐	BOUDOIR DOLLS ☐	MAMA DOLLS ☐
ANTIQUE LADY DOLLS ☐	CARNIVAL DOLLS ☐	MASK FACE DOLLS ☐
AUTOMATA DOLLS ☐	DRESS ME DOLLS ☐	ORIENTAL DOLLS ☐
BARBIE DOLLS ☐	GOOGLY EYE DOLLS ☐	PATSY TYPE DOLLS ☐
BLACK DOLLS ☐	KEWPIE DOLLS ☐	PORCELAIN COLLECTOR ☐

BY MATERIAL

BISQUE ☐	COMPOSITION ☐	RUBBER ☐
CELLULOID ☐	HARD PLASTIC ☐	WAX ☐
CHINA ☐	METAL ☐	WOOD ☐
CLOTH ☐	PAPIER MACHE ☐	

BY COUNTRY

AMERICAN ☐	FRENCH ☐	REST OF WORLD ☐
ENGLISH ☐	GERMAN ☐	

ADDITIONAL NOTES

_____

_____

_____

_____

ADD A PHOTO

BASIC INFORMATIONS

DOLL NAME	COUNTRY OF ORIGIN
MANUFACTURER	YEAR OF PRODUCTION
PURCHASE ☐	GIFT ☐
PURCHASE FROM	GIFT FROM
PURCHASE DATE	GIFT DATE

MARKINGS AND LABELS

MANUFACTURER STAMP
☐ YES ☐ NO

MODEL NUMBER
☐ YES ☐ NO

SYMBOL
☐ YES ☐ NO

CONDITION

IT HAS BEEN RESTORED OR REPAIR   YES ☐ NO ☐

CHIPPED   YES ☐ NO ☐   DULL   YES ☐ NO ☐   OTHER SIGNS OF WEAR   YES ☐ NO ☐

COST_____   CURRENT VALUE _____   RARENESS ☆☆☆☆☆

CERTIFICATE OF AUTHENTICITY   YES ☐ NO ☐

CHARACTERISTICS

HEAD_____   HEIGHT_____   ARMS_____

EYE STYLE_____   WEIGHT_____   BODY/SKIN_____

EYE COLOR_____   MOTION_____   HAIR COLOR_____

HAIR TYPE

CARACUL (WOOL) ☐

HUMAN HAIR ☐

MOHAIR ☐

SYNTHETIC HAIR ☐

YARN HAIR ☐

CLOTHES

CLOTHING STYLE_____   FABRIC_____

ACCESSORIES_____

DESCRIPTION OF CLOTHING_____

_____

DOLL CATEGORY

BY TYPE

ADVERTISING DOLLS	☐	BOUDOIR DOLLS	☐	MAMA DOLLS	☐
ANTIQUE LADY DOLLS	☐	CARNIVAL DOLLS	☐	MASK FACE DOLLS	☐
AUTOMATA DOLLS	☐	DRESS ME DOLLS	☐	ORIENTAL DOLLS	☐
BARBIE DOLLS	☐	GOOGLY EYE DOLLS	☐	PATSY TYPE DOLLS	☐
BLACK DOLLS	☐	KEWPIE DOLLS	☐	PORCELAIN COLLECTOR	☐

BY MATERIAL

BISQUE	☐	COMPOSITION	☐	RUBBER	☐
CELLULOID	☐	HARD PLASTIC	☐	WAX	☐
CHINA	☐	METAL	☐	WOOD	☐
CLOTH	☐	PAPIER MACHE	☐		

BY COUNTRY

AMERICAN	☐	FRENCH	☐	REST OF WORLD	☐
ENGLISH	☐	GERMAN	☐		

ADDITIONAL NOTES

_____

_____

_____

_____

ADD A PHOTO

BASIC INFORMATIONS

DOLL NAME	COUNTRY OF ORIGIN
MANUFACTURER	YEAR OF PRODUCTION
PURCHASE ☐	GIFT ☐
PURCHASE FROM	GIFT FROM
PURCHASE DATE	GIFT DATE

MARKINGS AND LABELS

MANUFACTURER STAMP
☐ YES   ☐ NO

MODEL NUMBER
☐ YES ☐ NO

SYMBOL
☐ YES ☐ NO

CONDITION

IT HAS BEEN RESTORED OR REPAIR   YES ☐   NO ☐

CHIPPED   YES ☐   NO ☐   DULL   YES ☐   NO ☐   OTHER SIGNS OF WEAR   YES ☐   NO ☐

COST_____   CURRENT VALUE _____   RARENESS ☆☆☆☆☆

CERTIFICATE OF AUTHENTICITY   YES ☐   NO ☐

CHARACTERISTICS

HEAD_____   HEIGHT_____   ARMS_____

EYE STYLE_____   WEIGHT_____   BODY/SKIN_____

EYE COLOR_____   MOTION_____   HAIR COLOR_____

HAIR TYPE

CARACUL (WOOL) ☐

HUMAN HAIR ☐

MOHAIR ☐

SYNTHETIC HAIR ☐

YARN HAIR ☐

CLOTHES

CLOTHING STYLE_____   FABRIC_____

ACCESSORIES_____

DESCRIPTION OF CLOTHING_____

_____

DOLL CATEGORY

BY TYPE

ADVERTISING DOLLS ☐	BOUDOIR DOLLS ☐	MAMA DOLLS ☐
ANTIQUE LADY DOLLS ☐	CARNIVAL DOLLS ☐	MASK FACE DOLLS ☐
AUTOMATA DOLLS ☐	DRESS ME DOLLS ☐	ORIENTAL DOLLS ☐
BARBIE DOLLS ☐	GOOGLY EYE DOLLS ☐	PATSY TYPE DOLLS ☐
BLACK DOLLS ☐	KEWPIE DOLLS ☐	PORCELAIN COLLECTOR ☐

BY MATERIAL

BISQUE ☐	COMPOSITION ☐	RUBBER ☐
CELLULOID ☐	HARD PLASTIC ☐	WAX ☐
CHINA ☐	METAL ☐	WOOD ☐
CLOTH ☐	PAPIER MACHE ☐	

BY COUNTRY

AMERICAN ☐	FRENCH ☐	REST OF WORLD ☐
ENGLISH ☐	GERMAN ☐	

ADDITIONAL NOTES

_____

_____

_____

_____

ADD A PHOTO

BASIC INFORMATIONS

DOLL NAME	COUNTRY OF ORIGIN
MANUFACTURER	YEAR OF PRODUCTION
PURCHASE ☐	GIFT ☐
PURCHASE FROM	GIFT FROM
PURCHASE DATE	GIFT DATE

MARKINGS AND LABELS

MANUFACTURER STAMP
☐ YES ☐ NO

MODEL NUMBER
☐ YES ☐ NO

SYMBOL
☐ YES ☐ NO

CONDITION

IT HAS BEEN RESTORED OR REPAIR   YES ☐ NO ☐

CHIPPED   YES ☐ NO ☐   DULL   YES ☐ NO ☐   OTHER SIGNS OF WEAR   YES ☐ NO ☐

COST_____   CURRENT VALUE _____   RARENESS ☆☆☆☆☆

CERTIFICATE OF AUTHENTICITY   YES ☐ NO ☐

CHARACTERISTICS

HEAD_____   HEIGHT_____   ARMS_____

EYE STYLE_____   WEIGHT_____   BODY/SKIN_____

EYE COLOR_____   MOTION_____   HAIR COLOR_____

HAIR TYPE

CARACUL (WOOL)   ☐

HUMAN HAIR   ☐

MOHAIR   ☐

SYNTHETIC HAIR   ☐

YARN HAIR   ☐

CLOTHES

CLOTHING STYLE_____   FABRIC_____

ACCESSORIES_____

DESCRIPTION OF CLOTHING_____

_____

DOLL CATEGORY

BY TYPE

ADVERTISING DOLLS ☐	BOUDOIR DOLLS ☐	MAMA DOLLS ☐
ANTIQUE LADY DOLLS ☐	CARNIVAL DOLLS ☐	MASK FACE DOLLS ☐
AUTOMATA DOLLS ☐	DRESS ME DOLLS ☐	ORIENTAL DOLLS ☐
BARBIE DOLLS ☐	GOOGLY EYE DOLLS ☐	PATSY TYPE DOLLS ☐
BLACK DOLLS ☐	KEWPIE DOLLS ☐	PORCELAIN COLLECTOR ☐

BY MATERIAL

BISQUE ☐	COMPOSITION ☐	RUBBER ☐
CELLULOID ☐	HARD PLASTIC ☐	WAX ☐
CHINA ☐	METAL ☐	WOOD ☐
CLOTH ☐	PAPIER MACHE ☐	

BY COUNTRY

AMERICAN ☐	FRENCH ☐	REST OF WORLD ☐
ENGLISH ☐	GERMAN ☐	

ADDITIONAL NOTES

_____

_____

_____

_____

ADD A PHOTO

BASIC INFORMATIONS

DOLL NAME	COUNTRY OF ORIGIN
MANUFACTURER	YEAR OF PRODUCTION
PURCHASE ☐	GIFT ☐
PURCHASE FROM	GIFT FROM
PURCHASE DATE	GIFT DATE

MARKINGS AND LABELS

MANUFACTURER STAMP
☐ YES   ☐ NO

MODEL NUMBER
☐ YES ☐ NO

SYMBOL
☐ YES   ☐ NO

CONDITION

IT HAS BEEN RESTORED OR REPAIR YES ☐ NO ☐

CHIPPED YES ☐ NO ☐   DULL YES ☐ NO ☐   OTHER SIGNS OF WEAR YES ☐ NO ☐

COST_____   CURRENT VALUE _____   RARENESS ☆☆☆☆☆

CERTIFICATE OF AUTHENTICITY YES ☐ NO ☐

CHARACTERISTICS

HEAD_____   HEIGHT_____   ARMS_____

EYE STYLE_____   WEIGHT_____   BODY/SKIN_____

EYE COLOR_____   MOTION_____   HAIR COLOR_____

HAIR TYPE

CARACUL (WOOL) ☐

HUMAN HAIR ☐

MOHAIR ☐

SYNTHETIC HAIR ☐

YARN HAIR ☐

CLOTHES

CLOTHING STYLE_____   FABRIC_____

ACCESSORIES_____

DESCRIPTION OF CLOTHING_____

_____

DOLL CATEGORY

BY TYPE

ADVERTISING DOLLS ☐	BOUDOIR DOLLS ☐	MAMA DOLLS ☐
ANTIQUE LADY DOLLS ☐	CARNIVAL DOLLS ☐	MASK FACE DOLLS ☐
AUTOMATA DOLLS ☐	DRESS ME DOLLS ☐	ORIENTAL DOLLS ☐
BARBIE DOLLS ☐	GOOGLY EYE DOLLS ☐	PATSY TYPE DOLLS ☐
BLACK DOLLS ☐	KEWPIE DOLLS ☐	PORCELAIN COLLECTOR ☐

BY MATERIAL

BISQUE ☐	COMPOSITION ☐	RUBBER ☐
CELLULOID ☐	HARD PLASTIC ☐	WAX ☐
CHINA ☐	METAL ☐	WOOD ☐
CLOTH ☐	PAPIER MACHE ☐	

BY COUNTRY

AMERICAN ☐	FRENCH ☐	REST OF WORLD ☐
ENGLISH ☐	GERMAN ☐	

ADDITIONAL NOTES

_____

_____

_____

_____

ADD A PHOTO

BASIC INFORMATIONS

DOLL NAME	COUNTRY OF ORIGIN
MANUFACTURER	YEAR OF PRODUCTION
PURCHASE ☐	GIFT ☐
PURCHASE FROM	GIFT FROM
PURCHASE DATE	GIFT DATE

MARKINGS AND LABELS

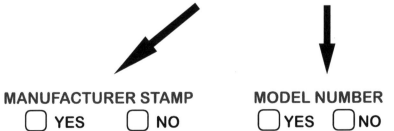

MANUFACTURER STAMP
☐ YES ☐ NO

MODEL NUMBER
☐ YES ☐ NO

SYMBOL
☐ YES ☐ NO

CONDITION

IT HAS BEEN RESTORED OR REPAIR YES ☐ NO ☐

CHIPPED YES ☐ NO ☐   DULL YES ☐ NO ☐   OTHER SIGNS OF WEAR YES ☐ NO ☐

COST_____   CURRENT VALUE _____   RARENESS ☆☆☆☆☆

CERTIFICATE OF AUTHENTICITY YES ☐ NO ☐

CHARACTERISTICS

HEAD_____   HEIGHT_____   ARMS_____

EYE STYLE_____   WEIGHT_____   BODY/SKIN_____

EYE COLOR_____   MOTION_____   HAIR COLOR_____

HAIR TYPE

CARACUL (WOOL) ☐

HUMAN HAIR ☐

MOHAIR ☐

SYNTHETIC HAIR ☐

YARN HAIR ☐

CLOTHES

CLOTHING STYLE_____   FABRIC_____

ACCESSORIES_____

DESCRIPTION OF CLOTHING_____

_____

DOLL CATEGORY

BY TYPE

ADVERTISING DOLLS ☐	BOUDOIR DOLLS ☐	MAMA DOLLS ☐
ANTIQUE LADY DOLLS ☐	CARNIVAL DOLLS ☐	MASK FACE DOLLS ☐
AUTOMATA DOLLS ☐	DRESS ME DOLLS ☐	ORIENTAL DOLLS ☐
BARBIE DOLLS ☐	GOOGLY EYE DOLLS ☐	PATSY TYPE DOLLS ☐
BLACK DOLLS ☐	KEWPIE DOLLS ☐	PORCELAIN COLLECTOR ☐

BY MATERIAL

BISQUE ☐	COMPOSITION ☐	RUBBER ☐
CELLULOID ☐	HARD PLASTIC ☐	WAX ☐
CHINA ☐	METAL ☐	WOOD ☐
CLOTH ☐	PAPIER MACHE ☐	

BY COUNTRY

AMERICAN ☐	FRENCH ☐	REST OF WORLD ☐
ENGLISH ☐	GERMAN ☐	

ADDITIONAL NOTES

_____

_____

_____

_____

ADD A PHOTO

BASIC INFORMATIONS

DOLL NAME	COUNTRY OF ORIGIN
MANUFACTURER	YEAR OF PRODUCTION
PURCHASE ☐	GIFT ☐
PURCHASE FROM	GIFT FROM
PURCHASE DATE	GIFT DATE

MARKINGS AND LABELS

MANUFACTURER STAMP
☐ YES ☐ NO

MODEL NUMBER
☐ YES ☐ NO

SYMBOL
☐ YES ☐ NO

CONDITION

IT HAS BEEN RESTORED OR REPAIR YES ☐ NO ☐

CHIPPED YES ☐ NO ☐   DULL YES ☐ NO ☐   OTHER SIGNS OF WEAR YES ☐ NO ☐

COST_____   CURRENT VALUE _____   RARENESS ☆☆☆☆☆

CERTIFICATE OF AUTHENTICITY YES ☐ NO ☐

CHARACTERISTICS

HEAD_____   HEIGHT_____   ARMS_____

EYE STYLE_____   WEIGHT_____   BODY/SKIN_____

EYE COLOR_____   MOTION_____   HAIR COLOR_____

HAIR TYPE

CARACUL (WOOL) ☐

HUMAN HAIR ☐

MOHAIR ☐

SYNTHETIC HAIR ☐

YARN HAIR ☐

CLOTHES

CLOTHING STYLE_____   FABRIC_____

ACCESSORIES_____

DESCRIPTION OF CLOTHING_____
_____

DOLL CATEGORY

BY TYPE

ADVERTISING DOLLS ☐	BOUDOIR DOLLS ☐	MAMA DOLLS ☐
ANTIQUE LADY DOLLS ☐	CARNIVAL DOLLS ☐	MASK FACE DOLLS ☐
AUTOMATA DOLLS ☐	DRESS ME DOLLS ☐	ORIENTAL DOLLS ☐
BARBIE DOLLS ☐	GOOGLY EYE DOLLS ☐	PATSY TYPE DOLLS ☐
BLACK DOLLS ☐	KEWPIE DOLLS ☐	PORCELAIN COLLECTOR ☐

BY MATERIAL

BISQUE ☐	COMPOSITION ☐	RUBBER ☐
CELLULOID ☐	HARD PLASTIC ☐	WAX ☐
CHINA ☐	METAL ☐	WOOD ☐
CLOTH ☐	PAPIER MACHE ☐	

BY COUNTRY

AMERICAN ☐	FRENCH ☐	REST OF WORLD ☐
ENGLISH ☐	GERMAN ☐	

ADDITIONAL NOTES

_____

_____

_____

_____

ADD A PHOTO

BASIC INFORMATIONS

DOLL NAME	COUNTRY OF ORIGIN
MANUFACTURER	YEAR OF PRODUCTION
PURCHASE ☐	GIFT ☐
PURCHASE FROM	GIFT FROM
PURCHASE DATE	GIFT DATE

MARKINGS AND LABELS

MANUFACTURER STAMP
☐ YES   ☐ NO

MODEL NUMBER
☐ YES   ☐ NO

SYMBOL
☐ YES   ☐ NO

CONDITION

IT HAS BEEN RESTORED OR REPAIR YES ☐ NO ☐

CHIPPED YES ☐ NO ☐   DULL YES ☐ NO ☐   OTHER SIGNS OF WEAR YES ☐ NO ☐

COST_____   CURRENT VALUE _____   RARENESS ☆☆☆☆☆

CERTIFICATE OF AUTHENTICITY YES ☐ NO ☐

CHARACTERISTICS

HEAD_____   HEIGHT_____   ARMS_____

EYE STYLE_____   WEIGHT_____   BODY/SKIN_____

EYE COLOR_____   MOTION_____   HAIR COLOR_____

HAIR TYPE

CARACUL (WOOL) ☐

HUMAN HAIR ☐

MOHAIR ☐

SYNTHETIC HAIR ☐

YARN HAIR ☐

CLOTHES

CLOTHING STYLE_____   FABRIC_____

ACCESSORIES_____

DESCRIPTION OF CLOTHING_____

_____

DOLL CATEGORY

BY TYPE

ADVERTISING DOLLS ☐	BOUDOIR DOLLS ☐	MAMA DOLLS ☐
ANTIQUE LADY DOLLS ☐	CARNIVAL DOLLS ☐	MASK FACE DOLLS ☐
AUTOMATA DOLLS ☐	DRESS ME DOLLS ☐	ORIENTAL DOLLS ☐
BARBIE DOLLS ☐	GOOGLY EYE DOLLS ☐	PATSY TYPE DOLLS ☐
BLACK DOLLS ☐	KEWPIE DOLLS ☐	PORCELAIN COLLECTOR ☐

BY MATERIAL

BISQUE ☐	COMPOSITION ☐	RUBBER ☐
CELLULOID ☐	HARD PLASTIC ☐	WAX ☐
CHINA ☐	METAL ☐	WOOD ☐
CLOTH ☐	PAPIER MACHE ☐	

BY COUNTRY

AMERICAN ☐	FRENCH ☐	REST OF WORLD ☐
ENGLISH ☐	GERMAN ☐	

ADDITIONAL NOTES

_____

_____

_____

_____

ADD A PHOTO

BASIC INFORMATIONS

DOLL NAME	**COUNTRY OF ORIGIN**
MANUFACTURER	**YEAR OF PRODUCTION**
PURCHASE ☐	**GIFT** ☐
PURCHASE FROM	**GIFT FROM**
PURCHASE DATE	**GIFT DATE**

MARKINGS AND LABELS

MANUFACTURER STAMP
 ☐ YES ☐ NO

MODEL NUMBER
 ☐ YES ☐ NO

SYMBOL
☐ YES ☐ NO

CONDITION

IT HAS BEEN RESTORED OR REPAIR   YES ☐ NO ☐

CHIPPED YES ☐ NO ☐   DULL YES ☐ NO ☐   OTHER SIGNS OF WEAR YES ☐ NO ☐

COST_____   CURRENT VALUE _____   RARENESS ☆☆☆☆☆

CERTIFICATE OF AUTHENTICITY   YES ☐ NO ☐

CHARACTERISTICS

HEAD_____   HEIGHT_____   ARMS_____

EYE STYLE_____   WEIGHT_____   BODY/SKIN_____

EYE COLOR_____   MOTION_____   HAIR COLOR_____

HAIR TYPE

CARACUL (WOOL) ☐

HUMAN HAIR ☐

MOHAIR ☐

SYNTHETIC HAIR ☐

YARN HAIR ☐

CLOTHES

CLOTHING STYLE_____   FABRIC_____

ACCESSORIES_____

DESCRIPTION OF CLOTHING_____

_____

DOLL CATEGORY

BY TYPE

ADVERTISING DOLLS ☐	BOUDOIR DOLLS ☐	MAMA DOLLS ☐
ANTIQUE LADY DOLLS ☐	CARNIVAL DOLLS ☐	MASK FACE DOLLS ☐
AUTOMATA DOLLS ☐	DRESS ME DOLLS ☐	ORIENTAL DOLLS ☐
BARBIE DOLLS ☐	GOOGLY EYE DOLLS ☐	PATSY TYPE DOLLS ☐
BLACK DOLLS ☐	KEWPIE DOLLS ☐	PORCELAIN COLLECTOR ☐

BY MATERIAL

BISQUE ☐	COMPOSITION ☐	RUBBER ☐
CELLULOID ☐	HARD PLASTIC ☐	WAX ☐
CHINA ☐	METAL ☐	WOOD ☐
CLOTH ☐	PAPIER MACHE ☐	

BY COUNTRY

AMERICAN ☐	FRENCH ☐	REST OF WORLD ☐
ENGLISH ☐	GERMAN ☐	

ADDITIONAL NOTES

_____

_____

_____

_____

ADD A PHOTO

BASIC INFORMATIONS

DOLL NAME	COUNTRY OF ORIGIN
MANUFACTURER	YEAR OF PRODUCTION
PURCHASE ☐	GIFT ☐
PURCHASE FROM	GIFT FROM
PURCHASE DATE	GIFT DATE

MARKINGS AND LABELS

MANUFACTURER STAMP
☐ YES   ☐ NO

MODEL NUMBER
☐ YES ☐ NO

SYMBOL
☐ YES ☐ NO

CONDITION

IT HAS BEEN RESTORED OR REPAIR
YES ☐ NO ☐

CHIPPED YES ☐ NO ☐   DULL YES ☐ NO ☐   OTHER SIGNS OF WEAR YES ☐ NO ☐

COST_____   CURRENT VALUE _____   RARENESS ☆☆☆☆☆

CERTIFICATE OF AUTHENTICITY YES ☐ NO ☐

CHARACTERISTICS

HEAD_____   HEIGHT_____   ARMS_____

EYE STYLE_____   WEIGHT_____   BODY/SKIN_____

EYE COLOR_____   MOTION_____   HAIR COLOR_____

HAIR TYPE

CARACUL (WOOL) ☐

HUMAN HAIR ☐

MOHAIR ☐

SYNTHETIC HAIR ☐

YARN HAIR ☐

CLOTHES

CLOTHING STYLE_____   FABRIC_____

ACCESSORIES_____

DESCRIPTION OF CLOTHING_____

_____

DOLL CATEGORY

BY TYPE

ADVERTISING DOLLS	☐	BOUDOIR DOLLS	☐	MAMA DOLLS	☐
ANTIQUE LADY DOLLS	☐	CARNIVAL DOLLS	☐	MASK FACE DOLLS	☐
AUTOMATA DOLLS	☐	DRESS ME DOLLS	☐	ORIENTAL DOLLS	☐
BARBIE DOLLS	☐	GOOGLY EYE DOLLS	☐	PATSY TYPE DOLLS	☐
BLACK DOLLS	☐	KEWPIE DOLLS	☐	PORCELAIN COLLECTOR	☐

BY MATERIAL

BISQUE	☐	COMPOSITION	☐	RUBBER	☐
CELLULOID	☐	HARD PLASTIC	☐	WAX	☐
CHINA	☐	METAL	☐	WOOD	☐
CLOTH	☐	PAPIER MACHE	☐		

BY COUNTRY

AMERICAN	☐	FRENCH	☐	REST OF WORLD	☐
ENGLISH	☐	GERMAN	☐		

ADDITIONAL NOTES

_____

_____

_____

_____

ADD A PHOTO

BASIC INFORMATIONS

DOLL NAME	COUNTRY OF ORIGIN
MANUFACTURER	YEAR OF PRODUCTION
PURCHASE ☐	GIFT ☐
PURCHASE FROM	GIFT FROM
PURCHASE DATE	GIFT DATE

MARKINGS AND LABELS

MANUFACTURER STAMP
☐ YES ☐ NO

MODEL NUMBER
☐ YES ☐ NO

SYMBOL
☐ YES ☐ NO

CONDITION

IT HAS BEEN RESTORED OR REPAIR YES ☐ NO ☐

CHIPPED YES ☐ NO ☐   DULL YES ☐ NO ☐   OTHER SIGNS OF WEAR YES ☐ NO ☐

COST_____   CURRENT VALUE _____   RARENESS ☆☆☆☆☆

CERTIFICATE OF AUTHENTICITY YES ☐ NO ☐

CHARACTERISTICS

HEAD_____   HEIGHT_____   ARMS_____

EYE STYLE_____   WEIGHT_____   BODY/SKIN_____

EYE COLOR_____   MOTION_____   HAIR COLOR_____

HAIR TYPE

CARACUL (WOOL) ☐

HUMAN HAIR ☐

MOHAIR ☐

SYNTHETIC HAIR ☐

YARN HAIR ☐

CLOTHES

CLOTHING STYLE_____   FABRIC_____

ACCESSORIES_____

DESCRIPTION OF CLOTHING_____

_____

DOLL CATEGORY

BY TYPE

ADVERTISING DOLLS ☐	BOUDOIR DOLLS ☐	MAMA DOLLS ☐
ANTIQUE LADY DOLLS ☐	CARNIVAL DOLLS ☐	MASK FACE DOLLS ☐
AUTOMATA DOLLS ☐	DRESS ME DOLLS ☐	ORIENTAL DOLLS ☐
BARBIE DOLLS ☐	GOOGLY EYE DOLLS ☐	PATSY TYPE DOLLS ☐
BLACK DOLLS ☐	KEWPIE DOLLS ☐	PORCELAIN COLLECTOR ☐

BY MATERIAL

BISQUE ☐	COMPOSITION ☐	RUBBER ☐
CELLULOID ☐	HARD PLASTIC ☐	WAX ☐
CHINA ☐	METAL ☐	WOOD ☐
CLOTH ☐	PAPIER MACHE ☐	

BY COUNTRY

AMERICAN ☐	FRENCH ☐	REST OF WORLD ☐
ENGLISH ☐	GERMAN ☐	

ADDITIONAL NOTES

_____

_____

_____

_____

ADD A PHOTO

BASIC INFORMATIONS

DOLL NAME	COUNTRY OF ORIGIN
MANUFACTURER	YEAR OF PRODUCTION
PURCHASE ☐	GIFT ☐
PURCHASE FROM	GIFT FROM
PURCHASE DATE	GIFT DATE

MARKINGS AND LABELS

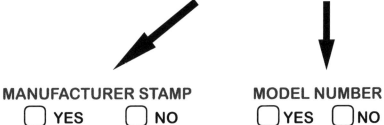

MANUFACTURER STAMP
☐ YES ☐ NO

MODEL NUMBER
☐ YES ☐ NO

SYMBOL
☐ YES ☐ NO

CONDITION

IT HAS BEEN RESTORED OR REPAIR   YES ☐   NO ☐

CHIPPED   YES ☐   NO ☐   DULL   YES ☐   NO ☐   OTHER SIGNS OF WEAR   YES ☐   NO ☐

COST_____   CURRENT VALUE _____   RARENESS ☆☆☆☆☆

CERTIFICATE OF AUTHENTICITY   YES ☐   NO ☐

CHARACTERISTICS

HEAD_____   HEIGHT_____   ARMS_____

EYE STYLE_____   WEIGHT_____   BODY/SKIN_____

EYE COLOR_____   MOTION_____   HAIR COLOR_____

HAIR TYPE

CARACUL (WOOL) ☐

HUMAN HAIR ☐

MOHAIR ☐

SYNTHETIC HAIR ☐

YARN HAIR ☐

CLOTHES

CLOTHING STYLE_____   FABRIC_____

ACCESSORIES_____

DESCRIPTION OF CLOTHING_____

_____

DOLL CATEGORY

BY TYPE

ADVERTISING DOLLS ☐	BOUDOIR DOLLS ☐	MAMA DOLLS ☐
ANTIQUE LADY DOLLS ☐	CARNIVAL DOLLS ☐	MASK FACE DOLLS ☐
AUTOMATA DOLLS ☐	DRESS ME DOLLS ☐	ORIENTAL DOLLS ☐
BARBIE DOLLS ☐	GOOGLY EYE DOLLS ☐	PATSY TYPE DOLLS ☐
BLACK DOLLS ☐	KEWPIE DOLLS ☐	PORCELAIN COLLECTOR ☐

BY MATERIAL

BISQUE ☐	COMPOSITION ☐	RUBBER ☐
CELLULOID ☐	HARD PLASTIC ☐	WAX ☐
CHINA ☐	METAL ☐	WOOD ☐
CLOTH ☐	PAPIER MACHE ☐	

BY COUNTRY

AMERICAN ☐	FRENCH ☐	REST OF WORLD ☐
ENGLISH ☐	GERMAN ☐	

ADDITIONAL NOTES

_____

_____

_____

_____

ADD A PHOTO

BASIC INFORMATIONS

DOLL NAME	COUNTRY OF ORIGIN
MANUFACTURER	YEAR OF PRODUCTION
PURCHASE ☐	GIFT ☐
PURCHASE FROM	GIFT FROM
PURCHASE DATE	GIFT DATE

MARKINGS AND LABELS

MANUFACTURER STAMP	MODEL NUMBER	SYMBOL
☐ YES ☐ NO	☐ YES ☐ NO	☐ YES ☐ NO

CONDITION

IT HAS BEEN RESTORED OR REPAIR   YES ☐ NO ☐

CHIPPED   YES ☐ NO ☐   DULL   YES ☐ NO ☐   OTHER SIGNS OF WEAR   YES ☐ NO ☐

COST_____   CURRENT VALUE _____   RARENESS ☆☆☆☆☆

CERTIFICATE OF AUTHENTICITY   YES ☐ NO ☐

CHARACTERISTICS

HEAD_____   HEIGHT_____   ARMS_____

EYE STYLE_____   WEIGHT_____   BODY/SKIN_____

EYE COLOR_____   MOTION_____   HAIR COLOR_____

HAIR TYPE

CARACUL (WOOL) ☐

HUMAN HAIR ☐

MOHAIR ☐

SYNTHETIC HAIR ☐

YARN HAIR ☐

CLOTHES

CLOTHING STYLE_____   FABRIC_____

ACCESSORIES_____

DESCRIPTION OF CLOTHING_____

_____

DOLL CATEGORY

BY TYPE

ADVERTISING DOLLS ☐	BOUDOIR DOLLS ☐	MAMA DOLLS ☐
ANTIQUE LADY DOLLS ☐	CARNIVAL DOLLS ☐	MASK FACE DOLLS ☐
AUTOMATA DOLLS ☐	DRESS ME DOLLS ☐	ORIENTAL DOLLS ☐
BARBIE DOLLS ☐	GOOGLY EYE DOLLS ☐	PATSY TYPE DOLLS ☐
BLACK DOLLS ☐	KEWPIE DOLLS ☐	PORCELAIN COLLECTOR ☐

BY MATERIAL

BISQUE ☐	COMPOSITION ☐	RUBBER ☐
CELLULOID ☐	HARD PLASTIC ☐	WAX ☐
CHINA ☐	METAL ☐	WOOD ☐
CLOTH ☐	PAPIER MACHE ☐	

BY COUNTRY

AMERICAN ☐	FRENCH ☐	REST OF WORLD ☐
ENGLISH ☐	GERMAN ☐	

ADDITIONAL NOTES

_____

_____

_____

_____

ADD A PHOTO

BASIC INFORMATIONS

DOLL NAME	COUNTRY OF ORIGIN
MANUFACTURER	YEAR OF PRODUCTION
PURCHASE ☐	GIFT ☐
PURCHASE FROM	GIFT FROM
PURCHASE DATE	GIFT DATE

MARKINGS AND LABELS

MANUFACTURER STAMP
☐ YES ☐ NO

MODEL NUMBER
☐ YES ☐ NO

SYMBOL
☐ YES ☐ NO

CONDITION

IT HAS BEEN RESTORED OR REPAIR   YES ☐   NO ☐

CHIPPED   YES ☐   NO ☐   DULL   YES ☐   NO ☐   OTHER SIGNS OF WEAR   YES ☐   NO ☐

COST_____   CURRENT VALUE _____   RARENESS ☆☆☆☆☆

CERTIFICATE OF AUTHENTICITY   YES ☐   NO ☐

CHARACTERISTICS

HEAD_____   HEIGHT_____   ARMS_____

EYE STYLE_____   WEIGHT_____   BODY/SKIN_____

EYE COLOR_____   MOTION_____   HAIR COLOR_____

HAIR TYPE

CARACUL (WOOL) ☐

HUMAN HAIR ☐

MOHAIR ☐

SYNTHETIC HAIR ☐

YARN HAIR ☐

CLOTHES

CLOTHING STYLE_____   FABRIC_____

ACCESSORIES_____

DESCRIPTION OF CLOTHING_____

_____

DOLL CATEGORY

BY TYPE

ADVERTISING DOLLS ☐	BOUDOIR DOLLS ☐	MAMA DOLLS ☐
ANTIQUE LADY DOLLS ☐	CARNIVAL DOLLS ☐	MASK FACE DOLLS ☐
AUTOMATA DOLLS ☐	DRESS ME DOLLS ☐	ORIENTAL DOLLS ☐
BARBIE DOLLS ☐	GOOGLY EYE DOLLS ☐	PATSY TYPE DOLLS ☐
BLACK DOLLS ☐	KEWPIE DOLLS ☐	PORCELAIN COLLECTOR ☐

BY MATERIAL

BISQUE ☐	COMPOSITION ☐	RUBBER ☐
CELLULOID ☐	HARD PLASTIC ☐	WAX ☐
CHINA ☐	METAL ☐	WOOD ☐
CLOTH ☐	PAPIER MACHE ☐	

BY COUNTRY

AMERICAN ☐	FRENCH ☐	REST OF WORLD ☐
ENGLISH ☐	GERMAN ☐	

ADDITIONAL NOTES

_____

_____

_____

_____

ADD A PHOTO

BASIC INFORMATIONS

DOLL NAME	COUNTRY OF ORIGIN
MANUFACTURER	YEAR OF PRODUCTION
PURCHASE ☐	GIFT ☐
PURCHASE FROM	GIFT FROM
PURCHASE DATE	GIFT DATE

MARKINGS AND LABELS

MANUFACTURER STAMP
☐ YES ☐ NO

MODEL NUMBER
☐ YES ☐ NO

SYMBOL
☐ YES ☐ NO

CONDITION

IT HAS BEEN RESTORED OR REPAIR YES ☐ NO ☐

CHIPPED YES ☐ NO ☐   DULL YES ☐ NO ☐   OTHER SIGNS OF WEAR YES ☐ NO ☐

COST_____   CURRENT VALUE _____   RARENESS ☆☆☆☆☆

CERTIFICATE OF AUTHENTICITY YES ☐ NO ☐

CHARACTERISTICS

HEAD_____   HEIGHT_____   ARMS_____

EYE STYLE_____   WEIGHT_____   BODY/SKIN_____

EYE COLOR_____   MOTION_____   HAIR COLOR_____

HAIR TYPE

CARACUL (WOOL) ☐

HUMAN HAIR ☐

MOHAIR ☐

SYNTHETIC HAIR ☐

YARN HAIR ☐

CLOTHES

CLOTHING STYLE_____   FABRIC_____

ACCESSORIES_____

DESCRIPTION OF CLOTHING_____

_____

DOLL CATEGORY

BY TYPE

ADVERTISING DOLLS ☐	BOUDOIR DOLLS ☐	MAMA DOLLS ☐
ANTIQUE LADY DOLLS ☐	CARNIVAL DOLLS ☐	MASK FACE DOLLS ☐
AUTOMATA DOLLS ☐	DRESS ME DOLLS ☐	ORIENTAL DOLLS ☐
BARBIE DOLLS ☐	GOOGLY EYE DOLLS ☐	PATSY TYPE DOLLS ☐
BLACK DOLLS ☐	KEWPIE DOLLS ☐	PORCELAIN COLLECTOR ☐

BY MATERIAL

BISQUE ☐	COMPOSITION ☐	RUBBER ☐
CELLULOID ☐	HARD PLASTIC ☐	WAX ☐
CHINA ☐	METAL ☐	WOOD ☐
CLOTH ☐	PAPIER MACHE ☐	

BY COUNTRY

AMERICAN ☐	FRENCH ☐	REST OF WORLD ☐
ENGLISH ☐	GERMAN ☐	

ADDITIONAL NOTES

_____

_____

_____

_____

ADD A PHOTO

BASIC INFORMATIONS

DOLL NAME	COUNTRY OF ORIGIN
MANUFACTURER	YEAR OF PRODUCTION
PURCHASE ☐	GIFT ☐
PURCHASE FROM	GIFT FROM
PURCHASE DATE	GIFT DATE

MARKINGS AND LABELS

MANUFACTURER STAMP
☐ YES   ☐ NO

MODEL NUMBER
☐ YES ☐ NO

SYMBOL
☐ YES ☐ NO

CONDITION

IT HAS BEEN RESTORED OR REPAIR YES ☐ NO ☐

CHIPPED YES ☐ NO ☐   DULL YES ☐ NO ☐   OTHER SIGNS OF WEAR YES ☐ NO ☐

COST_____   CURRENT VALUE _____   RARENESS ☆☆☆☆☆

CERTIFICATE OF AUTHENTICITY YES ☐ NO ☐

CHARACTERISTICS

HEAD_____   HEIGHT_____   ARMS_____

EYE STYLE_____   WEIGHT_____   BODY/SKIN_____

EYE COLOR_____   MOTION_____   HAIR COLOR_____

HAIR TYPE

CARACUL (WOOL) ☐

HUMAN HAIR ☐

MOHAIR ☐

SYNTHETIC HAIR ☐

YARN HAIR ☐

CLOTHES

CLOTHING STYLE_____   FABRIC_____

ACCESSORIES_____

DESCRIPTION OF CLOTHING_____

_____

DOLL CATEGORY

BY TYPE

ADVERTISING DOLLS	☐	BOUDOIR DOLLS	☐	MAMA DOLLS	☐
ANTIQUE LADY DOLLS	☐	CARNIVAL DOLLS	☐	MASK FACE DOLLS	☐
AUTOMATA DOLLS	☐	DRESS ME DOLLS	☐	ORIENTAL DOLLS	☐
BARBIE DOLLS	☐	GOOGLY EYE DOLLS	☐	PATSY TYPE DOLLS	☐
BLACK DOLLS	☐	KEWPIE DOLLS	☐	PORCELAIN COLLECTOR	☐

BY MATERIAL

BISQUE	☐	COMPOSITION	☐	RUBBER	☐
CELLULOID	☐	HARD PLASTIC	☐	WAX	☐
CHINA	☐	METAL	☐	WOOD	☐
CLOTH	☐	PAPIER MACHE	☐		

BY COUNTRY

AMERICAN	☐	FRENCH	☐	REST OF WORLD	☐
ENGLISH	☐	GERMAN	☐		

ADDITIONAL NOTES

_____

_____

_____

_____

ADD A PHOTO

BASIC INFORMATIONS

DOLL NAME	COUNTRY OF ORIGIN
MANUFACTURER	YEAR OF PRODUCTION
PURCHASE ☐	GIFT ☐
PURCHASE FROM	GIFT FROM
PURCHASE DATE	GIFT DATE

MARKINGS AND LABELS

MANUFACTURER STAMP
☐ YES   ☐ NO

MODEL NUMBER
☐ YES   ☐ NO

SYMBOL
☐ YES   ☐ NO

CONDITION

IT HAS BEEN RESTORED OR REPAIR   YES ☐ NO ☐

CHIPPED YES ☐ NO ☐   DULL YES ☐ NO ☐   OTHER SIGNS OF WEAR YES ☐ NO ☐

COST_____   CURRENT VALUE _____   RARENESS ☆☆☆☆☆

CERTIFICATE OF AUTHENTICITY   YES ☐ NO ☐

CHARACTERISTICS

HEAD_____   HEIGHT_____   ARMS_____

EYE STYLE_____   WEIGHT_____   BODY/SKIN_____

EYE COLOR_____   MOTION_____   HAIR COLOR_____

HAIR TYPE

CARACUL (WOOL) ☐

HUMAN HAIR ☐

MOHAIR ☐

SYNTHETIC HAIR ☐

YARN HAIR ☐

CLOTHES

CLOTHING STYLE_____   FABRIC_____

ACCESSORIES_____

DESCRIPTION OF CLOTHING_____

_____

DOLL CATEGORY

BY TYPE

ADVERTISING DOLLS ☐	BOUDOIR DOLLS ☐	MAMA DOLLS ☐
ANTIQUE LADY DOLLS ☐	CARNIVAL DOLLS ☐	MASK FACE DOLLS ☐
AUTOMATA DOLLS ☐	DRESS ME DOLLS ☐	ORIENTAL DOLLS ☐
BARBIE DOLLS ☐	GOOGLY EYE DOLLS ☐	PATSY TYPE DOLLS ☐
BLACK DOLLS ☐	KEWPIE DOLLS ☐	PORCELAIN COLLECTOR ☐

BY MATERIAL

BISQUE ☐	COMPOSITION ☐	RUBBER ☐
CELLULOID ☐	HARD PLASTIC ☐	WAX ☐
CHINA ☐	METAL ☐	WOOD ☐
CLOTH ☐	PAPIER MACHE ☐	

BY COUNTRY

AMERICAN ☐	FRENCH ☐	REST OF WORLD ☐
ENGLISH ☐	GERMAN ☐	

ADDITIONAL NOTES

_____

_____

_____

_____

ADD A PHOTO

BASIC INFORMATIONS

DOLL NAME	COUNTRY OF ORIGIN
MANUFACTURER	YEAR OF PRODUCTION
PURCHASE ☐	GIFT ☐
PURCHASE FROM	GIFT FROM
PURCHASE DATE	GIFT DATE

MARKINGS AND LABELS

MANUFACTURER STAMP
☐ YES   ☐ NO

MODEL NUMBER
☐ YES ☐ NO

SYMBOL
☐ YES ☐ NO

CONDITION

IT HAS BEEN RESTORED OR REPAIR YES ☐ NO ☐

CHIPPED YES ☐ NO ☐   DULL YES ☐ NO ☐   OTHER SIGNS OF WEAR YES ☐ NO ☐

COST_____   CURRENT VALUE _____   RARENESS ☆☆☆☆☆

CERTIFICATE OF AUTHENTICITY YES ☐ NO ☐

CHARACTERISTICS

HEAD_____   HEIGHT_____   ARMS_____

EYE STYLE_____   WEIGHT_____   BODY/SKIN_____

EYE COLOR_____   MOTION_____   HAIR COLOR_____

HAIR TYPE

CARACUL (WOOL) ☐

HUMAN HAIR ☐

MOHAIR ☐

SYNTHETIC HAIR ☐

YARN HAIR ☐

CLOTHES

CLOTHING STYLE_____   FABRIC_____

ACCESSORIES_____

DESCRIPTION OF CLOTHING_____

_____

DOLL CATEGORY

BY TYPE

ADVERTISING DOLLS	☐	BOUDOIR DOLLS	☐	MAMA DOLLS	☐
ANTIQUE LADY DOLLS	☐	CARNIVAL DOLLS	☐	MASK FACE DOLLS	☐
AUTOMATA DOLLS	☐	DRESS ME DOLLS	☐	ORIENTAL DOLLS	☐
BARBIE DOLLS	☐	GOOGLY EYE DOLLS	☐	PATSY TYPE DOLLS	☐
BLACK DOLLS	☐	KEWPIE DOLLS	☐	PORCELAIN COLLECTOR	☐

BY MATERIAL

BISQUE	☐	COMPOSITION	☐	RUBBER	☐
CELLULOID	☐	HARD PLASTIC	☐	WAX	☐
CHINA	☐	METAL	☐	WOOD	☐
CLOTH	☐	PAPIER MACHE	☐		

BY COUNTRY

AMERICAN	☐	FRENCH	☐	REST OF WORLD	☐
ENGLISH	☐	GERMAN	☐		

ADDITIONAL NOTES

_____

_____

_____

_____

ADD A PHOTO

BASIC INFORMATIONS

DOLL NAME		COUNTRY OF ORIGIN
MANUFACTURER		YEAR OF PRODUCTION
PURCHASE ☐		GIFT ☐
PURCHASE FROM		GIFT FROM
PURCHASE DATE		GIFT DATE

MARKINGS AND LABELS

MANUFACTURER STAMP
☐ YES   ☐ NO

MODEL NUMBER
☐ YES   ☐ NO

SYMBOL
☐ YES   ☐ NO

CONDITION

IT HAS BEEN RESTORED OR REPAIR YES ☐ NO ☐

CHIPPED YES ☐ NO ☐   DULL YES ☐ NO ☐   OTHER SIGNS OF WEAR YES ☐ NO ☐

COST_____   CURRENT VALUE _____   RARENESS ☆☆☆☆☆

CERTIFICATE OF AUTHENTICITY YES ☐ NO ☐

CHARACTERISTICS

HEAD_____   HEIGHT_____   ARMS_____

EYE STYLE_____   WEIGHT_____   BODY/SKIN_____

EYE COLOR_____   MOTION_____   HAIR COLOR_____

HAIR TYPE

CARACUL (WOOL) ☐

HUMAN HAIR ☐

MOHAIR ☐

SYNTHETIC HAIR ☐

YARN HAIR ☐

CLOTHES

CLOTHING STYLE_____   FABRIC_____

ACCESSORIES_____

DESCRIPTION OF CLOTHING_____

_____

DOLL CATEGORY

BY TYPE

ADVERTISING DOLLS ☐	BOUDOIR DOLLS ☐	MAMA DOLLS ☐
ANTIQUE LADY DOLLS ☐	CARNIVAL DOLLS ☐	MASK FACE DOLLS ☐
AUTOMATA DOLLS ☐	DRESS ME DOLLS ☐	ORIENTAL DOLLS ☐
BARBIE DOLLS ☐	GOOGLY EYE DOLLS ☐	PATSY TYPE DOLLS ☐
BLACK DOLLS ☐	KEWPIE DOLLS ☐	PORCELAIN COLLECTOR ☐

BY MATERIAL

BISQUE ☐	COMPOSITION ☐	RUBBER ☐
CELLULOID ☐	HARD PLASTIC ☐	WAX ☐
CHINA ☐	METAL ☐	WOOD ☐
CLOTH ☐	PAPIER MACHE ☐	

BY COUNTRY

AMERICAN ☐	FRENCH ☐	REST OF WORLD ☐
ENGLISH ☐	GERMAN ☐	

ADDITIONAL NOTES

_____

_____

_____

_____

ADD A PHOTO

BASIC INFORMATIONS

DOLL NAME	COUNTRY OF ORIGIN
MANUFACTURER	YEAR OF PRODUCTION
PURCHASE ☐	GIFT ☐
PURCHASE FROM	GIFT FROM
PURCHASE DATE	GIFT DATE

MARKINGS AND LABELS

MANUFACTURER STAMP
☐ YES   ☐ NO

MODEL NUMBER
☐ YES ☐ NO

SYMBOL
☐ YES   ☐ NO

CONDITION

IT HAS BEEN RESTORED OR REPAIR   YES ☐   NO ☐

CHIPPED   YES ☐   NO ☐   DULL   YES ☐   NO ☐   OTHER SIGNS OF WEAR   YES ☐   NO ☐

COST_____   CURRENT VALUE _____   RARENESS ☆☆☆☆☆

CERTIFICATE OF AUTHENTICITY   YES ☐   NO ☐

CHARACTERISTICS

HEAD_____   HEIGHT_____   ARMS_____

EYE STYLE_____   WEIGHT_____   BODY/SKIN_____

EYE COLOR_____   MOTION_____   HAIR COLOR_____

HAIR TYPE

CARACUL (WOOL) ☐

HUMAN HAIR ☐

MOHAIR ☐

SYNTHETIC HAIR ☐

YARN HAIR ☐

CLOTHES

CLOTHING STYLE_____   FABRIC_____

ACCESSORIES_____

DESCRIPTION OF CLOTHING_____

_____

DOLL CATEGORY

BY TYPE

ADVERTISING DOLLS ☐	BOUDOIR DOLLS ☐	MAMA DOLLS ☐
ANTIQUE LADY DOLLS ☐	CARNIVAL DOLLS ☐	MASK FACE DOLLS ☐
AUTOMATA DOLLS ☐	DRESS ME DOLLS ☐	ORIENTAL DOLLS ☐
BARBIE DOLLS ☐	GOOGLY EYE DOLLS ☐	PATSY TYPE DOLLS ☐
BLACK DOLLS ☐	KEWPIE DOLLS ☐	PORCELAIN COLLECTOR ☐

BY MATERIAL

BISQUE ☐	COMPOSITION ☐	RUBBER ☐
CELLULOID ☐	HARD PLASTIC ☐	WAX ☐
CHINA ☐	METAL ☐	WOOD ☐
CLOTH ☐	PAPIER MACHE ☐	

BY COUNTRY

AMERICAN ☐	FRENCH ☐	REST OF WORLD ☐
ENGLISH ☐	GERMAN ☐	

ADDITIONAL NOTES

_____

_____

_____

_____

ADD A PHOTO

BASIC INFORMATIONS

DOLL NAME	COUNTRY OF ORIGIN
MANUFACTURER	YEAR OF PRODUCTION
PURCHASE ☐	GIFT ☐
PURCHASE FROM	GIFT FROM
PURCHASE DATE	GIFT DATE

MARKINGS AND LABELS

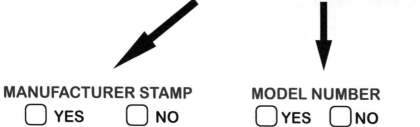

MANUFACTURER STAMP
☐ YES   ☐ NO

MODEL NUMBER
☐ YES   ☐ NO

SYMBOL
☐ YES   ☐ NO

CONDITION

IT HAS BEEN RESTORED OR REPAIR   YES ☐   NO ☐

CHIPPED   YES ☐   NO ☐   DULL   YES ☐   NO ☐   OTHER SIGNS OF WEAR   YES ☐   NO ☐

COST_____   CURRENT VALUE _____   RARENESS ☆☆☆☆☆

CERTIFICATE OF AUTHENTICITY   YES ☐   NO ☐

CHARACTERISTICS

HEAD_____   HEIGHT_____   ARMS_____

EYE STYLE_____   WEIGHT_____   BODY/SKIN_____

EYE COLOR_____   MOTION_____   HAIR COLOR_____

HAIR TYPE

CARACUL (WOOL) ☐

HUMAN HAIR ☐

MOHAIR ☐

SYNTHETIC HAIR ☐

YARN HAIR ☐

CLOTHES

CLOTHING STYLE_____   FABRIC_____

ACCESSORIES_____

DESCRIPTION OF CLOTHING_____

_____

DOLL CATEGORY

BY TYPE

ADVERTISING DOLLS ☐	BOUDOIR DOLLS ☐	MAMA DOLLS ☐
ANTIQUE LADY DOLLS ☐	CARNIVAL DOLLS ☐	MASK FACE DOLLS ☐
AUTOMATA DOLLS ☐	DRESS ME DOLLS ☐	ORIENTAL DOLLS ☐
BARBIE DOLLS ☐	GOOGLY EYE DOLLS ☐	PATSY TYPE DOLLS ☐
BLACK DOLLS ☐	KEWPIE DOLLS ☐	PORCELAIN COLLECTOR ☐

BY MATERIAL

BISQUE ☐	COMPOSITION ☐	RUBBER ☐
CELLULOID ☐	HARD PLASTIC ☐	WAX ☐
CHINA ☐	METAL ☐	WOOD ☐
CLOTH ☐	PAPIER MACHE ☐	

BY COUNTRY

AMERICAN ☐	FRENCH ☐	REST OF WORLD ☐
ENGLISH ☐	GERMAN ☐	

ADDITIONAL NOTES

_____

_____

_____

_____

ADD A PHOTO

BASIC INFORMATIONS

DOLL NAME	COUNTRY OF ORIGIN
MANUFACTURER	YEAR OF PRODUCTION
PURCHASE ☐	GIFT ☐
PURCHASE FROM	GIFT FROM
PURCHASE DATE	GIFT DATE

MARKINGS AND LABELS

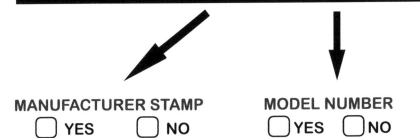

MANUFACTURER STAMP
☐ YES ☐ NO

MODEL NUMBER
☐ YES ☐ NO

SYMBOL
☐ YES ☐ NO

CONDITION

IT HAS BEEN RESTORED OR REPAIR   YES ☐ NO ☐

CHIPPED   YES ☐ NO ☐   DULL   YES ☐ NO ☐   OTHER SIGNS OF WEAR   YES ☐ NO ☐

COST_____   CURRENT VALUE_____   RARENESS ☆☆☆☆☆

CERTIFICATE OF AUTHENTICITY   YES ☐ NO ☐

CHARACTERISTICS

HEAD_____   HEIGHT_____   ARMS_____

EYE STYLE_____   WEIGHT_____   BODY/SKIN_____

EYE COLOR_____   MOTION_____   HAIR COLOR_____

HAIR TYPE

CARACUL (WOOL)   ☐

HUMAN HAIR   ☐

MOHAIR   ☐

SYNTHETIC HAIR   ☐

YARN HAIR   ☐

CLOTHES

CLOTHING STYLE_____   FABRIC_____

ACCESSORIES_____

DESCRIPTION OF CLOTHING_____

_____

DOLL CATEGORY

BY TYPE

ADVERTISING DOLLS ☐	BOUDOIR DOLLS ☐	MAMA DOLLS ☐
ANTIQUE LADY DOLLS ☐	CARNIVAL DOLLS ☐	MASK FACE DOLLS ☐
AUTOMATA DOLLS ☐	DRESS ME DOLLS ☐	ORIENTAL DOLLS ☐
BARBIE DOLLS ☐	GOOGLY EYE DOLLS ☐	PATSY TYPE DOLLS ☐
BLACK DOLLS ☐	KEWPIE DOLLS ☐	PORCELAIN COLLECTOR ☐

BY MATERIAL

BISQUE ☐	COMPOSITION ☐	RUBBER ☐
CELLULOID ☐	HARD PLASTIC ☐	WAX ☐
CHINA ☐	METAL ☐	WOOD ☐
CLOTH ☐	PAPIER MACHE ☐	

BY COUNTRY

AMERICAN ☐	FRENCH ☐	REST OF WORLD ☐
ENGLISH ☐	GERMAN ☐	

ADDITIONAL NOTES

_____

_____

_____

_____

ADD A PHOTO

BASIC INFORMATIONS

DOLL NAME	COUNTRY OF ORIGIN
MANUFACTURER	YEAR OF PRODUCTION
PURCHASE ☐	GIFT ☐
PURCHASE FROM	GIFT FROM
PURCHASE DATE	GIFT DATE

MARKINGS AND LABELS

MANUFACTURER STAMP
☐ YES   ☐ NO

MODEL NUMBER
☐ YES   ☐ NO

SYMBOL
☐ YES   ☐ NO

CONDITION

IT HAS BEEN RESTORED OR REPAIR
YES ☐ NO ☐

CHIPPED YES ☐ NO ☐   DULL YES ☐ NO ☐   OTHER SIGNS OF WEAR YES ☐ NO ☐

COST_____   CURRENT VALUE _____   RARENESS ☆☆☆☆☆

CERTIFICATE OF AUTHENTICITY YES ☐ NO ☐

CHARACTERISTICS

HEAD_____   HEIGHT_____   ARMS_____

EYE STYLE_____   WEIGHT_____   BODY/SKIN_____

EYE COLOR_____   MOTION_____   HAIR COLOR_____

HAIR TYPE

CARACUL (WOOL) ☐

HUMAN HAIR ☐

MOHAIR ☐

SYNTHETIC HAIR ☐

YARN HAIR ☐

CLOTHES

CLOTHING STYLE_____   FABRIC_____

ACCESSORIES_____

DESCRIPTION OF CLOTHING_____

_____

DOLL CATEGORY

BY TYPE

ADVERTISING DOLLS ☐	BOUDOIR DOLLS ☐	MAMA DOLLS ☐
ANTIQUE LADY DOLLS ☐	CARNIVAL DOLLS ☐	MASK FACE DOLLS ☐
AUTOMATA DOLLS ☐	DRESS ME DOLLS ☐	ORIENTAL DOLLS ☐
BARBIE DOLLS ☐	GOOGLY EYE DOLLS ☐	PATSY TYPE DOLLS ☐
BLACK DOLLS ☐	KEWPIE DOLLS ☐	PORCELAIN COLLECTOR ☐

BY MATERIAL

BISQUE ☐	COMPOSITION ☐	RUBBER ☐
CELLULOID ☐	HARD PLASTIC ☐	WAX ☐
CHINA ☐	METAL ☐	WOOD ☐
CLOTH ☐	PAPIER MACHE ☐	

BY COUNTRY

AMERICAN ☐	FRENCH ☐	REST OF WORLD ☐
ENGLISH ☐	GERMAN ☐	

ADDITIONAL NOTES

_____

_____

_____

_____

DOLL CATEGORY

BY TYPE

ADVERTISING DOLLS ☐	BOUDOIR DOLLS ☐	MAMA DOLLS ☐
ANTIQUE LADY DOLLS ☐	CARNIVAL DOLLS ☐	MASK FACE DOLLS ☐
AUTOMATA DOLLS ☐	DRESS ME DOLLS ☐	ORIENTAL DOLLS ☐
BARBIE DOLLS ☐	GOOGLY EYE DOLLS ☐	PATSY TYPE DOLLS ☐
BLACK DOLLS ☐	KEWPIE DOLLS ☐	PORCELAIN COLLECTOR ☐

BY MATERIAL

BISQUE ☐	COMPOSITION ☐	RUBBER ☐
CELLULOID ☐	HARD PLASTIC ☐	WAX ☐
CHINA ☐	METAL ☐	WOOD ☐
CLOTH ☐	PAPIER MACHE ☐	

BY COUNTRY

AMERICAN ☐	FRENCH ☐	REST OF WORLD ☐
ENGLISH ☐	GERMAN ☐	

ADDITIONAL NOTES

_____

_____

_____

_____

ADD A PHOTO

BASIC INFORMATIONS

DOLL NAME	COUNTRY OF ORIGIN
MANUFACTURER	YEAR OF PRODUCTION
PURCHASE ☐	GIFT ☐
PURCHASE FROM	GIFT FROM
PURCHASE DATE	GIFT DATE

MARKINGS AND LABELS

MANUFACTURER STAMP
☐ YES   ☐ NO

MODEL NUMBER
☐ YES   ☐ NO

SYMBOL
☐ YES   ☐ NO

CONDITION

IT HAS BEEN RESTORED OR REPAIR YES ☐ NO ☐

CHIPPED YES ☐ NO ☐   DULL YES ☐ NO ☐   OTHER SIGNS OF WEAR YES ☐ NO ☐

COST_____   CURRENT VALUE _____   RARENESS ☆☆☆☆☆

CERTIFICATE OF AUTHENTICITY YES ☐ NO ☐

CHARACTERISTICS

HEAD_____   HEIGHT_____   ARMS_____

EYE STYLE_____   WEIGHT_____   BODY/SKIN_____

EYE COLOR_____   MOTION_____   HAIR COLOR_____

HAIR TYPE

CARACUL (WOOL) ☐

HUMAN HAIR ☐

MOHAIR ☐

SYNTHETIC HAIR ☐

YARN HAIR ☐

CLOTHES

CLOTHING STYLE_____   FABRIC_____

ACCESSORIES_____

DESCRIPTION OF CLOTHING_____

_____

DOLL CATEGORY

BY TYPE

ADVERTISING DOLLS ☐	BOUDOIR DOLLS ☐	MAMA DOLLS ☐
ANTIQUE LADY DOLLS ☐	CARNIVAL DOLLS ☐	MASK FACE DOLLS ☐
AUTOMATA DOLLS ☐	DRESS ME DOLLS ☐	ORIENTAL DOLLS ☐
BARBIE DOLLS ☐	GOOGLY EYE DOLLS ☐	PATSY TYPE DOLLS ☐
BLACK DOLLS ☐	KEWPIE DOLLS ☐	PORCELAIN COLLECTOR ☐

BY MATERIAL

BISQUE ☐	COMPOSITION ☐	RUBBER ☐
CELLULOID ☐	HARD PLASTIC ☐	WAX ☐
CHINA ☐	METAL ☐	WOOD ☐
CLOTH ☐	PAPIER MACHE ☐	

BY COUNTRY

AMERICAN ☐	FRENCH ☐	REST OF WORLD ☐
ENGLISH ☐	GERMAN ☐	

ADDITIONAL NOTES

_____

_____

_____

_____

Made in the USA
Columbia, SC
18 June 2022